and all our Anchors...

~ *s.b. & a.s.*

Grew up with power boats, married a sailor and have taught all three children a healthy respect for both.

~ *s.b.*

Created and self-published by:
Sara Booker
4780 Hinckley Industrial Pkwy
Suite 200
Cleveland, OH 44109
sbooker43456@aol.com

Photographs taken by:
Audrey Sheehan & are located at
audreysheehan.com

Available for resale on amazon.com. & many local retailers
Visit our Facebook page for retail locations

Printing production by Bookmasters, Ashland, OH
Printed in the U.S.A. with pride!

All quotes, lyrics and written verse are quoted from original author or entertainer and are proudly used with respect to promote their artistic expression and craft. The written words on all pages in this book are property of the owners copyright, as their name or character appears beneath the printed words or stated in the Contributors & Credits. Every reasonable attempt has been made to identify owners of copyright. Errors or omissions will be corrected in subsequent editions.

*PIB, is the abbreviation for Put-in-Bay, a small resort town located on South Bass Island, one of the Lake Erie Islands. A true treasure & a must see on your bucket list!

ISBN: 978 0 692 02105 7
Library of Congress Control Number: 2014935015

B Break

O Out

A Another

T Thousand

Ships are the nearest things to dreams that hands have ever made.

Robert N. Rose

New York Harbor, NY

This land is your land, this land is my land,
From California, to the New York Island,
From the Redwood Forest, to the
Gulf Stream waters.
This land was made for you and me.

Woody Guthrie

The voice of the sea speaks to the soul...

Kate Chopin

Conch Shell

The wind and the waves are always on the side of the ablest navigator.

Edward Gibbon

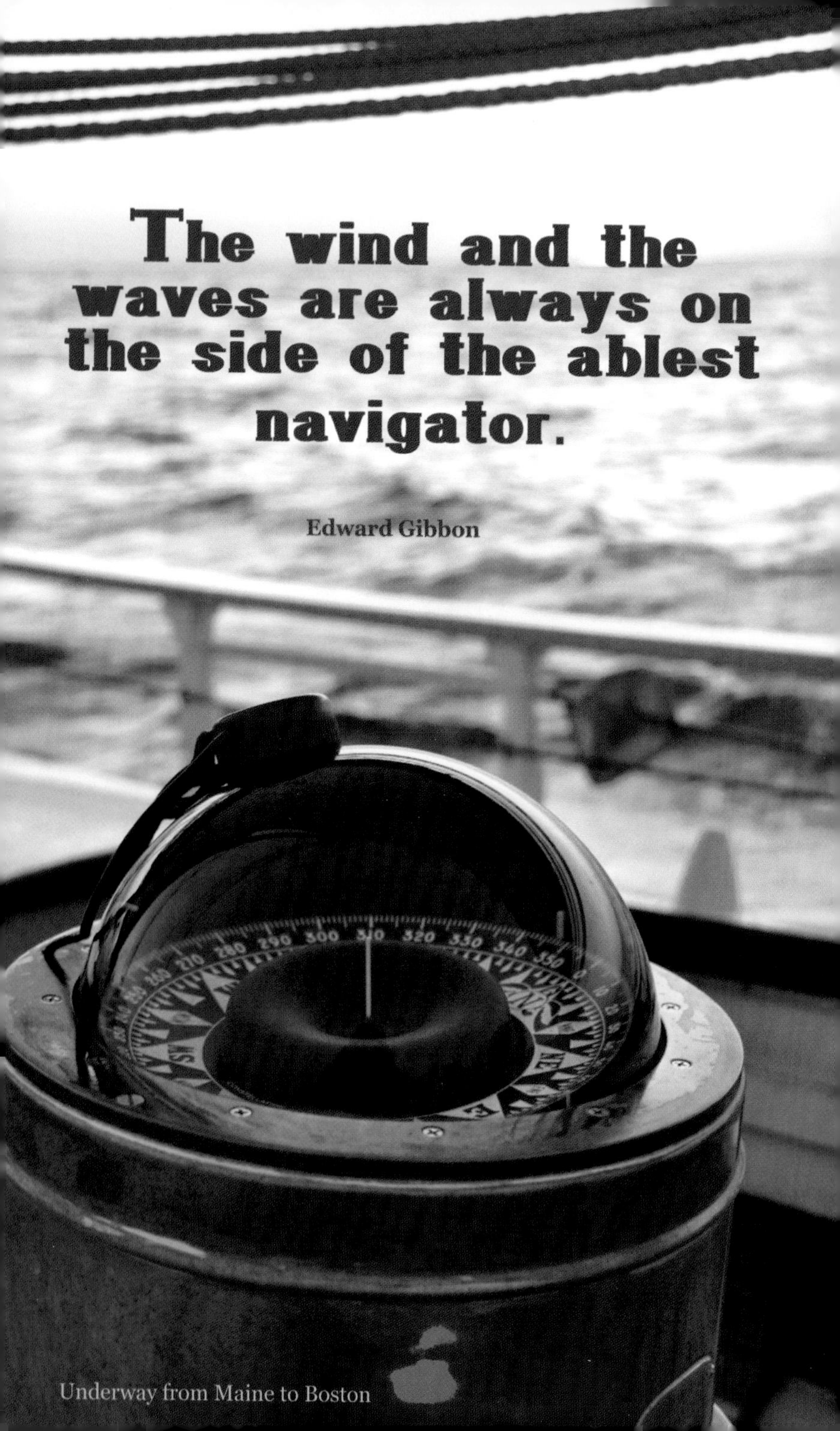

Underway from Maine to Boston

advice
from
the

OCEAN

Be Shore of Yourself
Come Out of Your Shell
Take Time to Coast
Avoid Pier Pressure
Sea Life's Beauty
Don't Get Tide Down
Make Waves!

Unknown

St. Eustatius,
Leeward Islands, West Indies

Please be reasonable and do it **MY** way!

THE CAPTAIN

Prevention is, as in other aspects of seamanship, better than cure.

Sir Robin Knox Johnston

BOARD THE FERRY
ACTIVATE ISLAND TIME
FORGET YOUR WORRIES
STAY FOR A WHILE

Sara Booker

Miller Boat Line, PIB, OH

Ferry Boats

Over the river,
Over the bay,
Ferry boats travel every day.

Most of the people
Crowd to the side
Just to enjoy
Their ferry boat ride.

Watching the seagulls,
Laughing with friends,
I'm always sorry
When the ride ends.

James S. Tippett

DON'T GIVE UP THE SHIP

James Lawrence

Star Spangled Banner

O say, can you see, by the dawn's early light, what so proudly we hail'd at the twilight's last gleaming? Whose broad stripes and bright stars, thro' the perilous fight, o'er the ramparts we watch'd, were so gallantly streaming? And the rockets' red glare, the bombs bursting in air, gave proof thro' the night that our flag was still there. O say, does that star-spangled banner yet wave o'er the land of the free and the home of the brave?

Francis Scott Key

Marina Cay, BVI

A drop in the ocean.
A change in the weather.
I was praying that you and me might end up together.

Ron Pope

HE WHO LETS THE SEA LULL HIM INTO A SENSE OF SECURITY IS IN VERY GRAVE DANGER

Hammond Innes

Caribbean Sea

Waves are not measured in feet or inches, they are measured in increments of fear.

Buzzy Trent

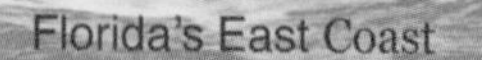

Florida's East Coast

The sea does not reward those who are too anxious, too greedy, or too impatient. One should lie empty, open choiceless as a beach- waiting for a

GIFT FROM THE SEA.

Anne Morrow Lindbergh

Just sit right back
And you'll hear a tale
A tale of a fateful trip,
That started from this tropic port,
Aboard this tiny ship.
The mate was a mighty sailin' man,
The Skipper brave and sure,
Five passengers set sail that day,
For a three hour tour,
A three hour tour.

The weather started getting rough,
The tiny ship was tossed.
If not for the courage of the fearless crew
The Minnow would be lost.
The Minnow would be lost.

Gilligan's Island

M.M. 88 Restaurant, Islamorada, FL

I must be a mermaid... for I have no fear of depths and great fear of shallow living.

Anais Nin

Hens & Chickens Reef, FL Keys
Photo: Jack Booker 13 yrs. old

And it is an interesting biological fact that all of us have, in our veins the exact same percentage of salt in our blood that exists in the ocean, and, therefore, we have salt in our blood, in our sweat, in our tears. We are tied to the ocean. And when we go back to the sea, whether it is to sail or to watch it, we are going back from whence we came.

John F. Kennedy

The Falls, Chagrin Falls, OH

Make no mistake. There is nothin' better than a day at the Lake!

Never a ship sails out of a bay, but carries my heart as a stowaway.

Roselle Mercier Montgomery

If a man is to be obsessed by something, I suppose a boat is as good as anything, perhaps a bit better than most.

E.B. White

A woman's heart is a deep ocean of secrets.

Rose, *Titanic* 1997

Cobh, Ireland

I'd much rather be a woman than a man. Women can cry, they can wear cute clothes, and they're the first to be rescued off sinking ships.

Gilda Radner

Seize the moment. Remember all those women on the "Titanic" who waved off the dessert cart.

Erma Bombeck

South Bass Island, OH

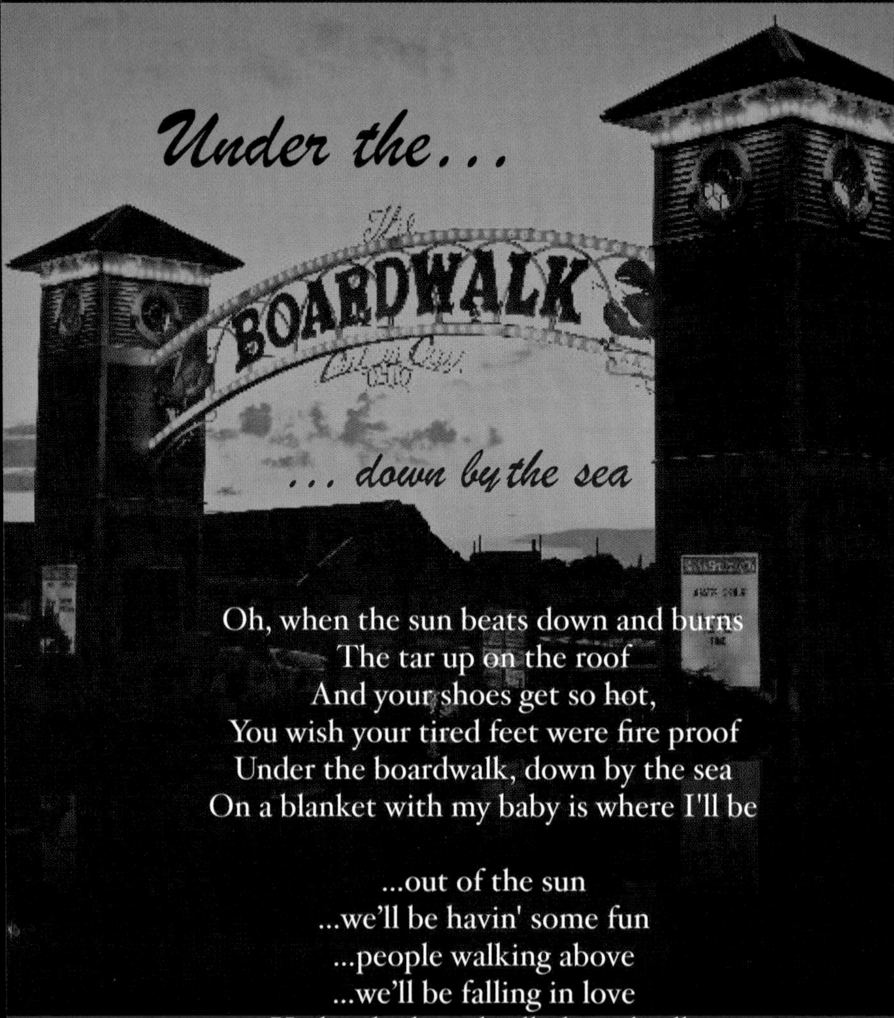

Under the...

BOARDWALK

... down by the sea

Oh, when the sun beats down and burns
The tar up on the roof
And your shoes get so hot,
You wish your tired feet were fire proof
Under the boardwalk, down by the sea
On a blanket with my baby is where I'll be

...out of the sun
...we'll be havin' some fun
...people walking above
...we'll be falling in love
Under the boardwalk, boardwalk

From the park you hear the happy sound of a carousel
You can almost taste the hot dogs and french fries they sell
Under the boardwalk, down by the sea,
On a blanket with my baby is where I'll be

Red sky by morning,

Sailor take warning.

Red sky at night,

Sailor's delight.

Old English Proverb

Trinidad Sunset

Now Bring Me That Horizon

Captain Jack Sparrow, *Pirates of the Caribbean*

Jolly boating weather,
and a hay harvest breeze, blade on the feather,
shade off the trees.

William Johnson Cory

Perdido Key, FL

All love that has not friendship for its base, is like a mansion built upon the sand.

Ella Wheeler Wilcox

My Heart is at Home by the Sea

Whenever your
preparations for
the sea are poor;
the sea worms its
way in and finds the
problems.

Francis Stokes

Antigua

There is nothing quite like a night on an island. From Put~in~Bay to The Keys, all islands, far and in-between.

Sara Booker

Key West, FL

The sea! The sea!
The open sea!
The blue, the fresh,
The ever free!

Barry Cornwall

IT'S MORE FUN TO BE A PIRATE THAN TO JOIN THE NAVY.

Steve Jobs

Why do ships use knots instead of miles?

To keep the sea tide.

Atlantic Ocean Sunset

Fort Berkeley, English Harbour, Antigua

Yo ho, yo ho, the frisky plank,

You walks along it so,

Till it goes down and you goes down

To Davy Jones below!

Captain Hook, *Peter Pan in Kensington Gardens*

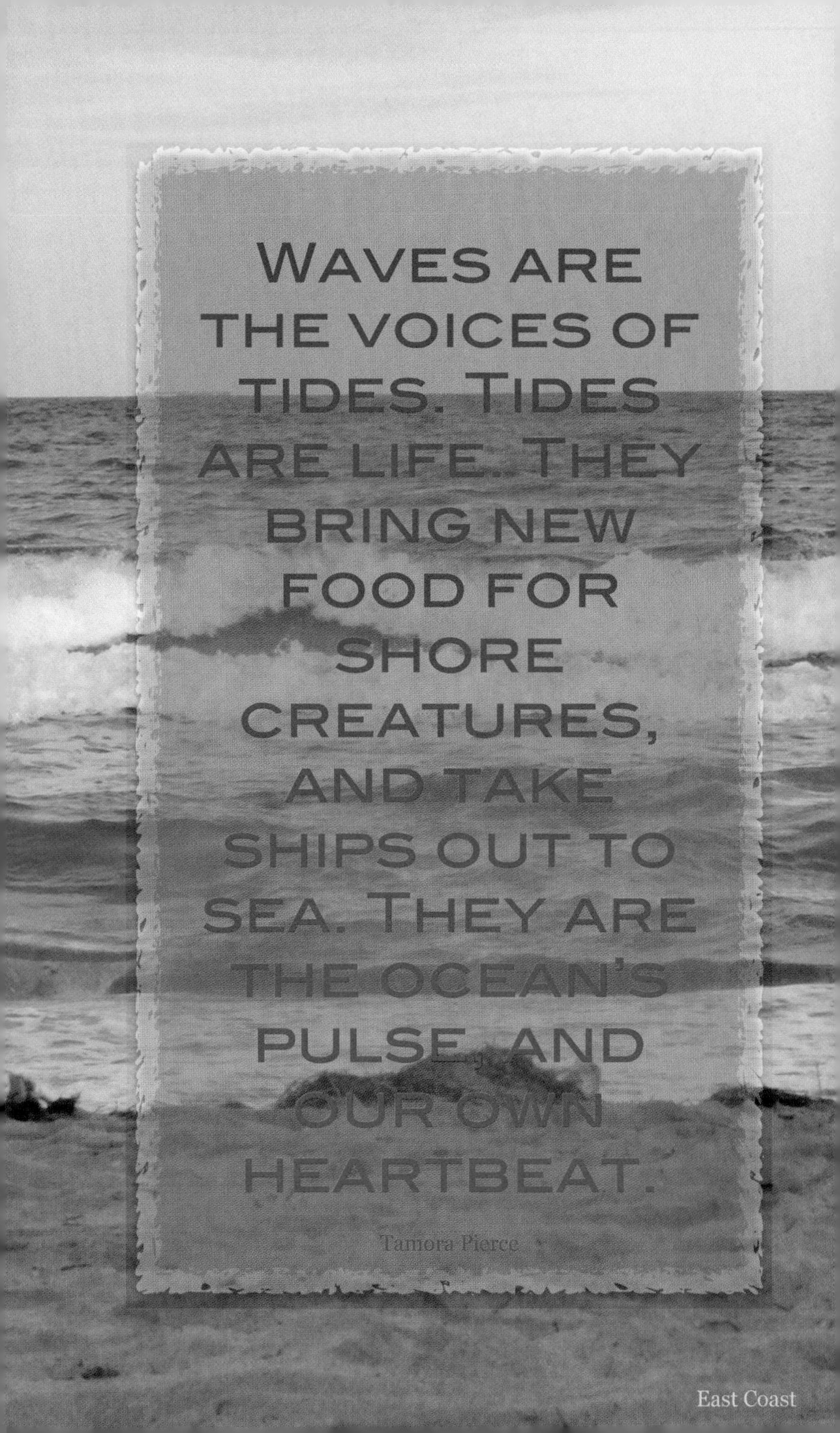
Waves are the voices of tides. Tides are life. They bring new food for shore creatures, and take ships out to sea. They are the ocean's pulse, and our own heartbeat.
Tamora Pierce
East Coast

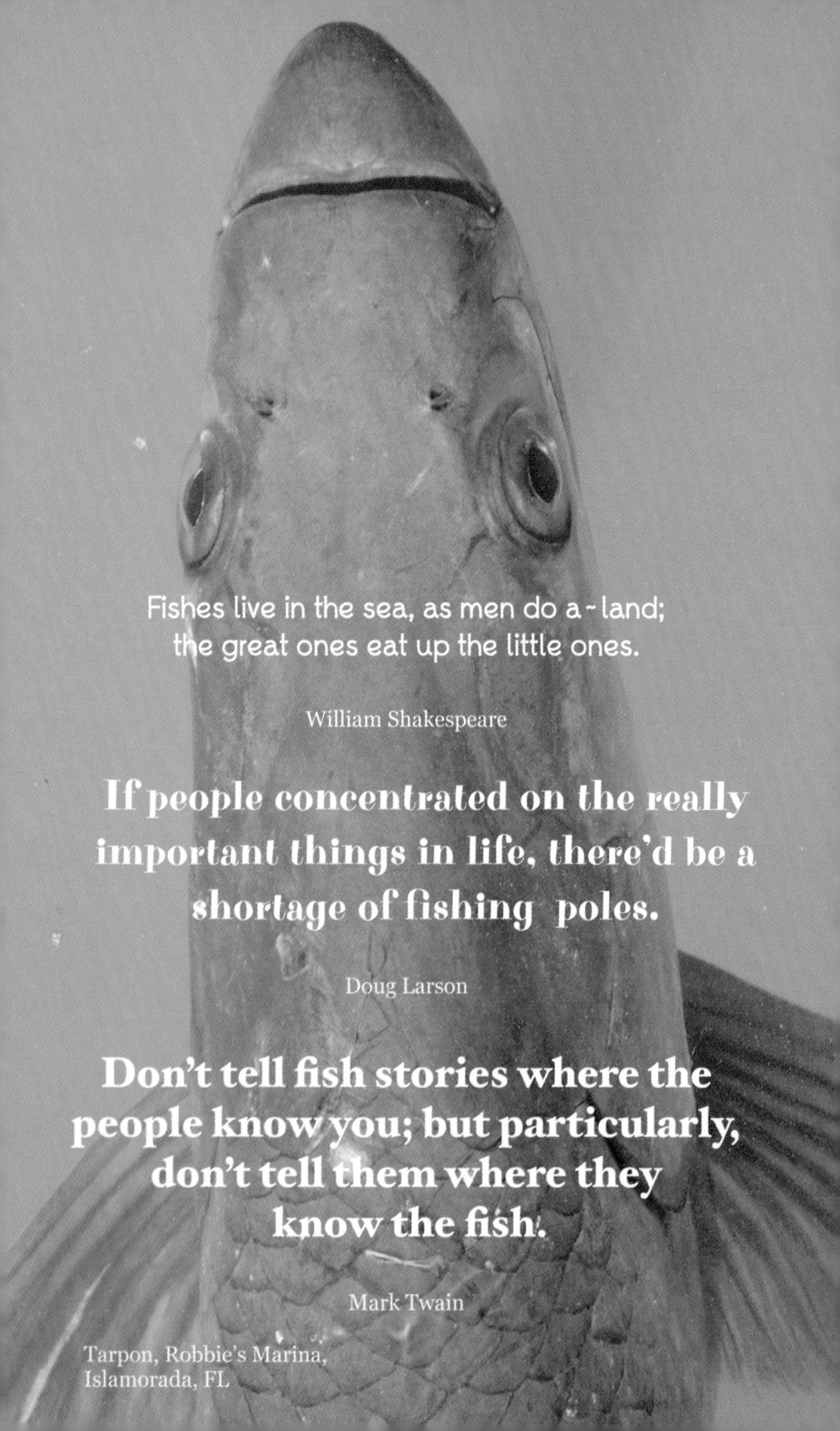

Fishes live in the sea, as men do a-land;
the great ones eat up the little ones.

William Shakespeare

If people concentrated on the really important things in life, there'd be a shortage of fishing poles.

Doug Larson

Don't tell fish stories where the people know you; but particularly, don't tell them where they know the fish.

Mark Twain

Tarpon, Robbie's Marina,
Islamorada, FL

Limitless and immortal, the waters are the beginning and the end of all things on earth.

Heinrich Zimmer

Honduras

Those who have one foot in the canoe, and one foot in the boat, are going to fall into the river.

Native American Wisdom

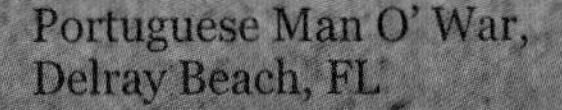

Portuguese Man O' War,
Delray Beach, FL

We've got to get right down to the sea
We've got to get to the sea

Jack Johnson

When the tides of life turn against you
and the current upsets your boat, don't
waste those tears on what might have
been, just lie on your back and float.

Unknown

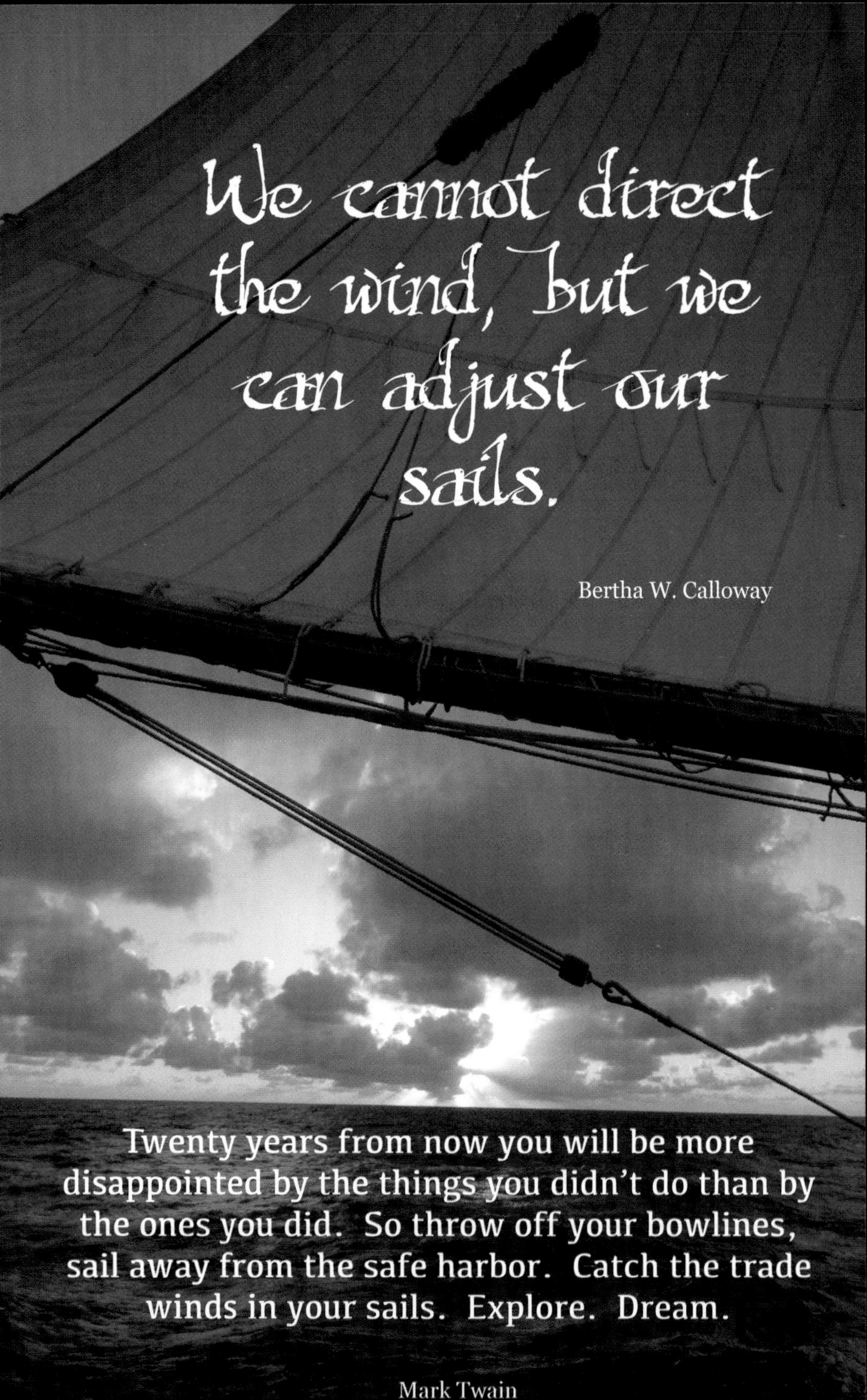

We cannot direct the wind, but we can adjust our sails.

Bertha W. Calloway

Twenty years from now you will be more disappointed by the things you didn't do than by the ones you did. So throw off your bowlines, sail away from the safe harbor. Catch the trade winds in your sails. Explore. Dream.

Mark Twain

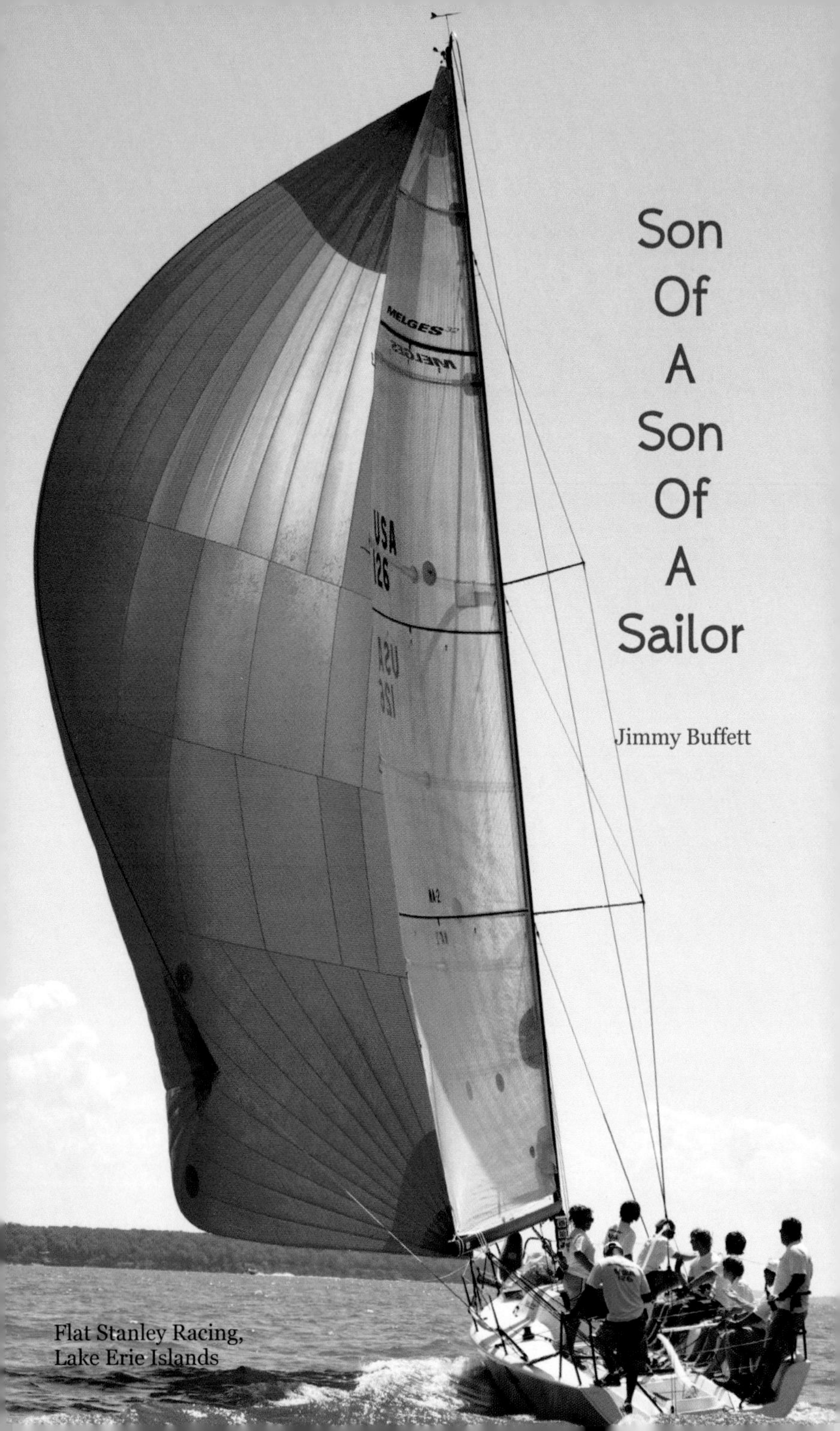

Son Of A Son Of A Sailor

Jimmy Buffett

Flat Stanley Racing,
Lake Erie Islands

The world is my *Lobster*.

Henry J. Tillman

Coast of Maine

A lobster walks into a bar…
The bartender says… Why the beady eyes?

How long does it take a
lobster to run a marathon?

A shell of a long time

Why did the lobster do so well at craps?

Because he was on a roll

Hanakapiai Beach, Kauai, HI

If there is magic
on this planet,
it is contained in water.

Loren Eiseley

ATTITUDE IS THE DIFFERENCE BETWEEN ORDEAL AND ADVENTURE.

Bob Bitchin

Sailing BVI

The joy of life comes from our encounters with new experiences. Hence there is no greater joy than to have an endlessly changing horizon, for each new day to have a different sun.

Chris McCandless

Lake Huron, MI

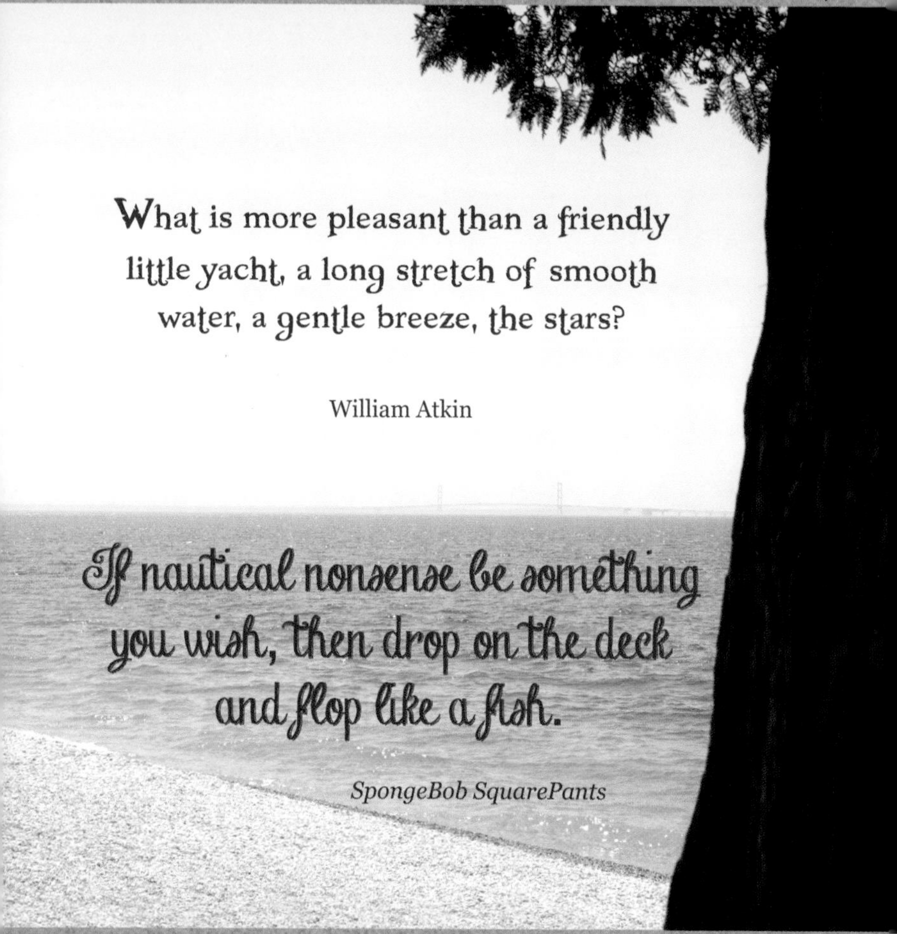

What is more pleasant than a friendly little yacht, a long stretch of smooth water, a gentle breeze, the stars?

William Atkin

If nautical nonsense be something you wish, then drop on the deck and flop like a fish.

SpongeBob SquarePants

Splashing through the sandbar,
talking by the campfire.
It's the simple things in life like when and where.
We didn't have no internet
but man I never will forget
the way the moonlight
shined upon her hair.

Kid Rock

Definitely not the
Great Lakes

Someday my ship will
come in, and with my
luck I'll be at the airport.

Thomas Hardy

I like big boats and I cannot lie.

Boats are just like tools…
Can you imagine having only one
tool in your tool box?

Anonymous

Protector's Samson Post

Mackerel skies and mares tails, soon
will be time to shorten sails.

Old Sailors Proverb

If you can't repair it, maybe
it shouldn't be on board.

Lin and L[illegible]ardey

Lighthouses are unique expressions of human creativity. Physically, they represent triumphant solutions to complex engineering problems. Emotionally, they exemplify drama, rescue, poetry, romance, grandeur, nostalgia, and artistry.

Charles Wysocki

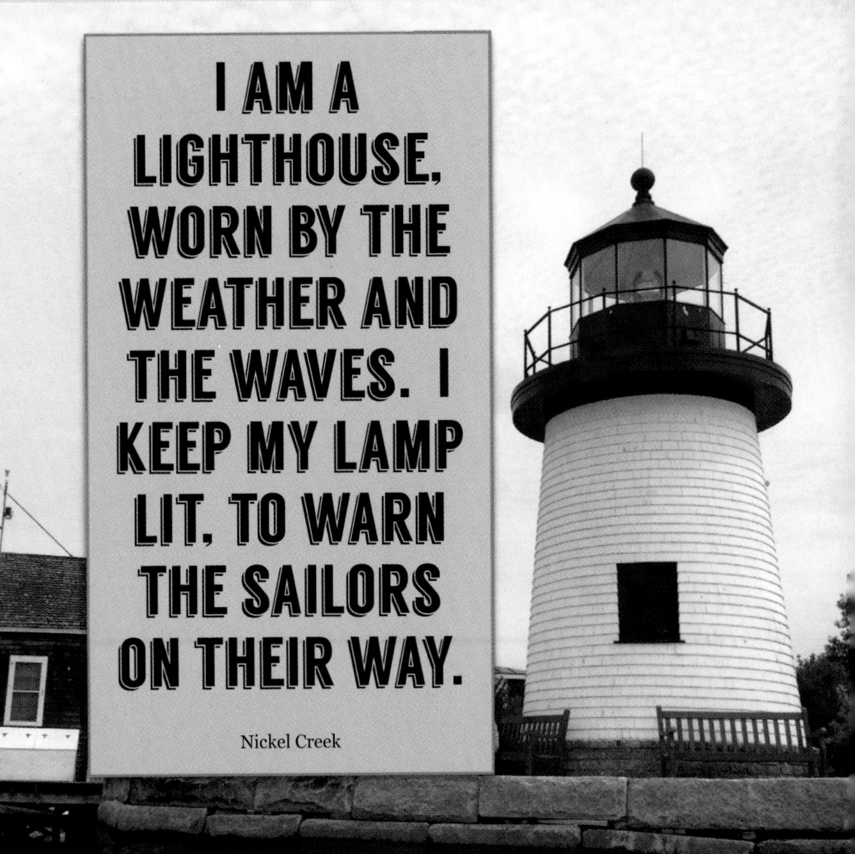

Mystic Seaport Historic Lighthouse, CT

I ARISE TODAY
THROUGH THE STRENGTH
OF HEAVEN;
LIGHT OF THE SUN,
SPLENDOR OF FIRE,
SPEED OF LIGHTNING,
SWIFTNESS OF THE WIND,
DEPTH OF THE SEA,
STABILITY OF THE EARTH,
FIRMNESS OF THE ROCK.

St. Partick

Largest Peninsula of the U.S.

Ride the Waves of Life

"Mom Down"
The Baths, Jost Van Dyke, BVI

The ocean old, Centuries old,
Strong as youth,
And as uncontrolled
Paces restless to and fro,
Up and down the sands of gold.

Henry Wadsworth Longfellow

Feelin' Knotty? Wine Knot...

Let's have a hull of a lotta fun!

Sally B.S.

If you can't tie a knot, tie a lot.

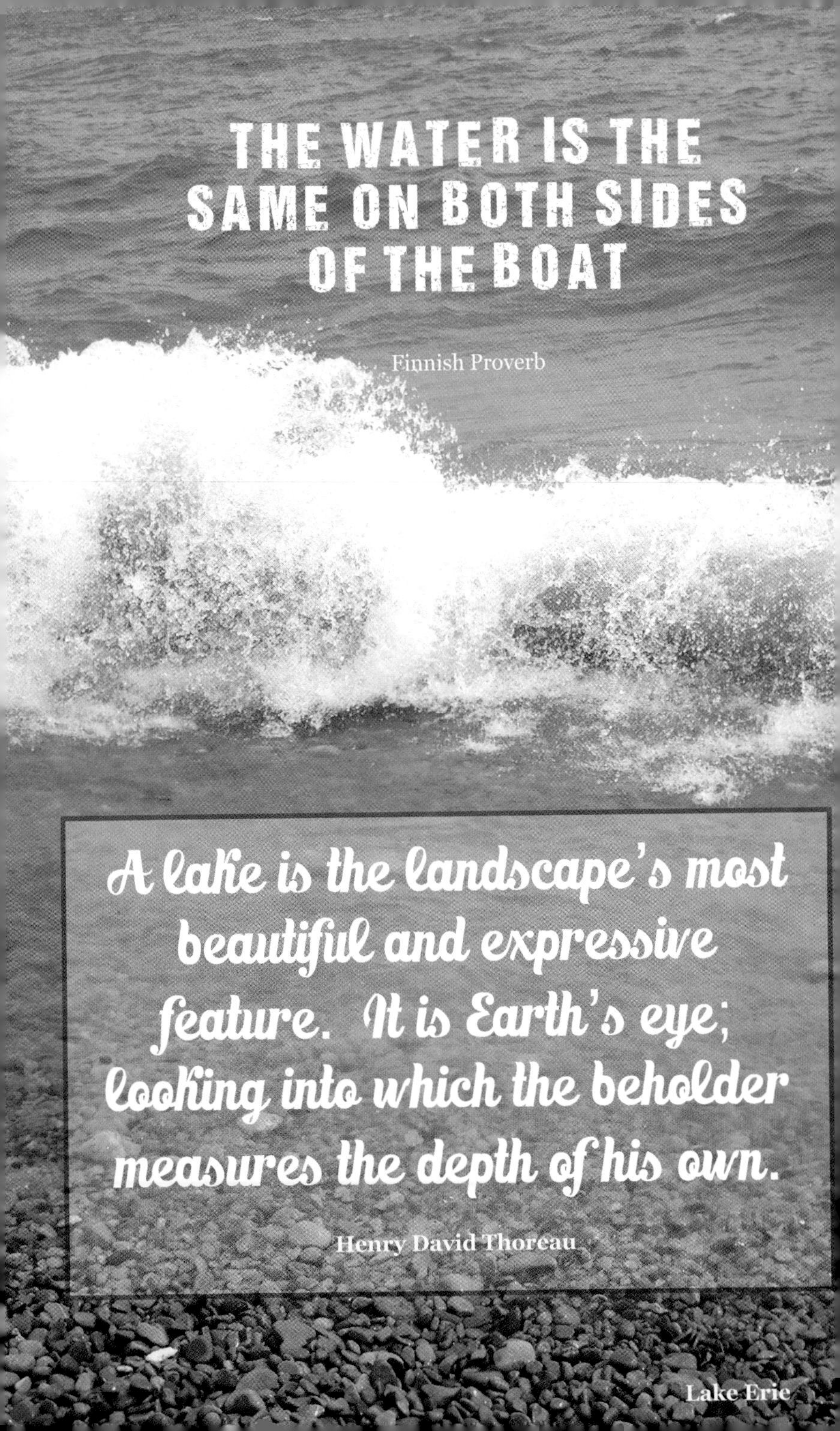

THE WATER IS THE SAME ON BOTH SIDES OF THE BOAT

Finnish Proverb

A lake is the landscape's most beautiful and expressive feature. It is Earth's eye; looking into which the beholder measures the depth of his own.

Henry David Thoreau

Lake Erie

Little Harbour, PIB, OH

There are some things you learn best in calm and some in storm

Willa Cather

You need to overcome the tug of people against you as you reach for high goals.

George S. Patton

Belize

Time and tide wait for no man, but always stand still for a woman of thirty...

Robert Frost

TO SAIL IS HUMAN.....TO POWER DIVINE!

Preben Sejer Kristensen

Well I'm on the Downeaster Alexa
And I'm cruising through Block Island Sound
I have charted a course to the Vineyard
But tonight I am Nantucket bound

We took on diesel back in Montauk yesterday
And left this morning from the bell in Gardiner's Bay
Like all the locals here I've had to sell my home
Too proud to leave I've worked my fingers to the bone

So I could own my Downeaster Alexa
And I go where the ocean is deep
There are giants out there in the canyons
And a good captain can't fall asleep

I've got bills to pay and children who need clothes
I know there's fish out there but where God only knows
They say these waters aren't what they used to be
But I've got people back on land who count on me

So if you see my Downeaster Alexa
And if you work with the rod and the reel
Tell my wife I am trawling Atlantis
And I still have my hands on the wheel

Now I drive my Downeaster Alexa
More and more miles from shore every year
Since they tell me I can't sell no stripers
And there's no luck in swordfishing here

I was a bayman like my father was before
Can't make a living as a bayman anymore
There ain't much future for a man who works the sea
But there ain't no island left for islanders like me

Billy Joel

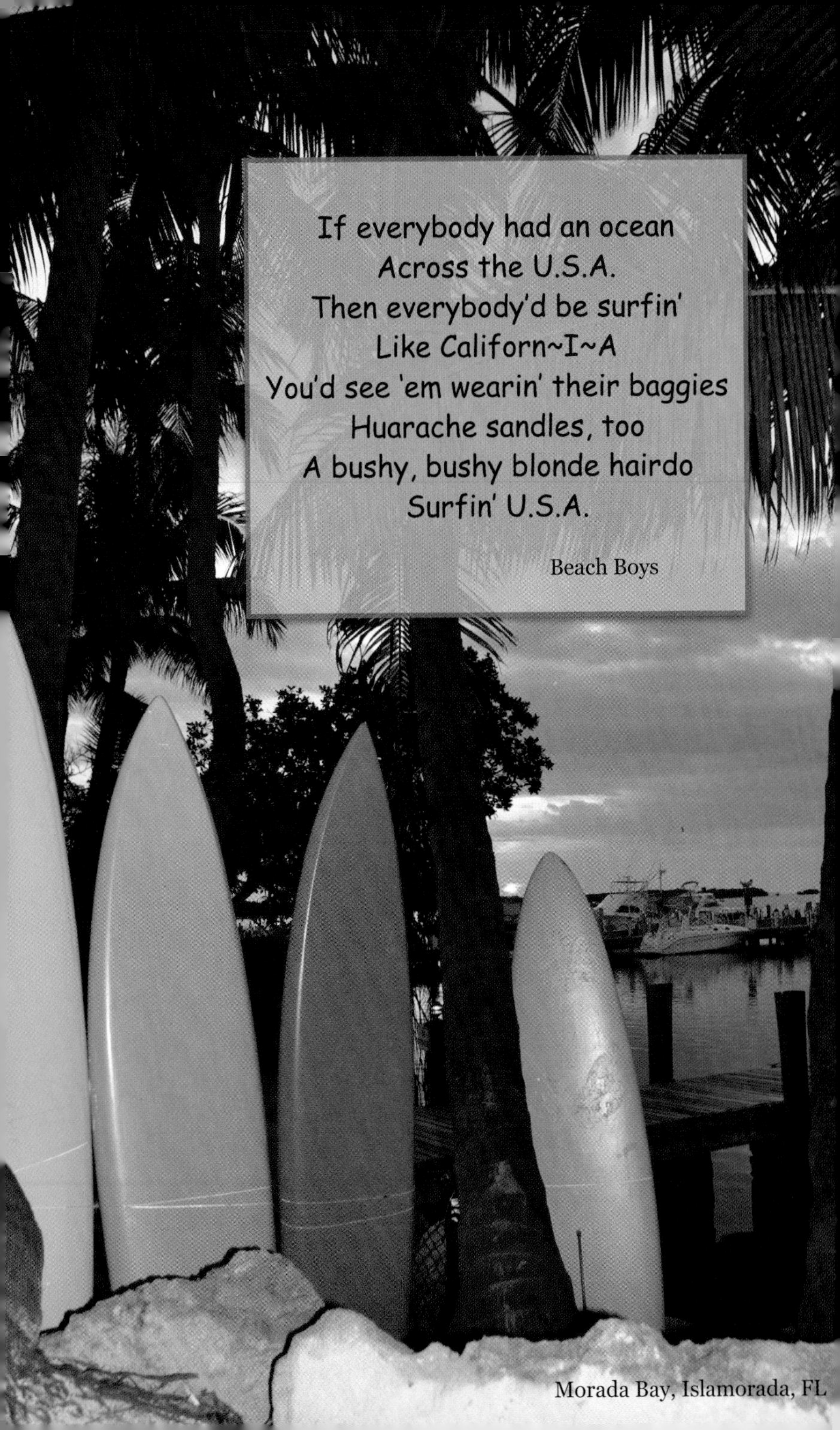

If everybody had an ocean
Across the U.S.A.
Then everybody'd be surfin'
Like Californ~I~A
You'd see 'em wearin' their baggies
Huarache sandles, too
A bushy, bushy blonde hairdo
Surfin' U.S.A.

Beach Boys

Morada Bay, Islamorada, FL

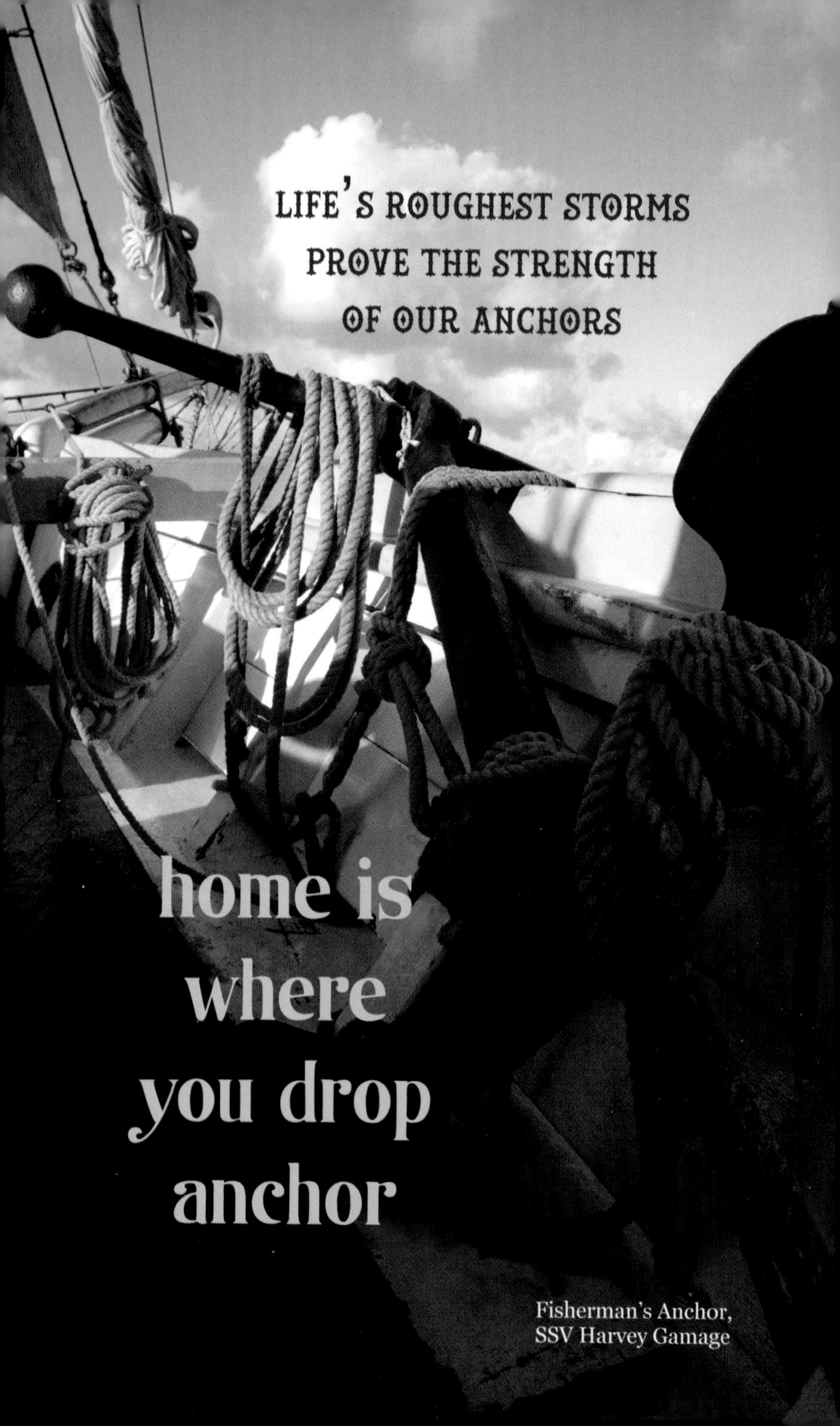

LIFE'S ROUGHEST STORMS
PROVE THE STRENGTH
OF OUR ANCHORS

home is
where
you drop
anchor

Fisherman's Anchor,
SSV Harvey Gamage

FISH ON!

Key West, FL

There are three sorts of people,
those who are Alive,
those who are Dead,
and those who are at Sea.

Anacharsis

One of the best temporary
cures for pride and
affection is seasickness.

Henry Wheeler Shaw

There's no such thing as bad weather, only bad clothes.

Old Norwegian Adage

SSV Harvey Gamage,
Underway for Guadeloupe

Call me Ishmael. Some years ago- never mind how long precisely- having little or no money in my purse, and nothing particular to interest me on shore, I thought I would sail about a little and see the watery part of the world.

Herman Melville, *Moby Dick*

Nassau, Bahamas

Brandy

There's a port on a western bay
And it serves a hundred ships a day
Lonely sailors pass the time away
And talk about their homes

And there's a girl in this harbor town
And she works layin' whiskey down
They say "Brandy, fetch another round"
She serves them whiskey and wine

The sailors say "Brandy, you're a fine girl"
"What a good wife you would be"
"Yeah your eyes could steal a sailor from the sea"

Looking Glass

Give a man a fish and he has food for a day;
teach him how to fish and you can
get rid of him for an entire weekend.

Zenna Schaffer

Key West, FL

Somebody just back of you while you are fishing is as bad as someone looking over your shoulder while you write a letter to your girl. Ernest Hemingway

Fishing is a discipline in the equality of men… for all men are equal before fish. Herbert Hoover

Approaching Antigua

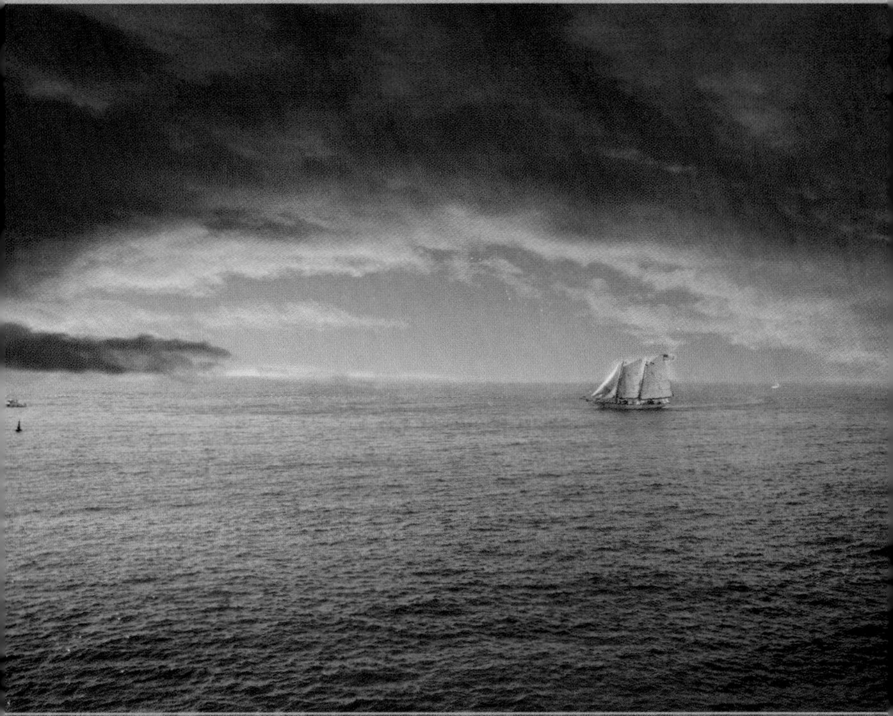

I must go down to the sea again,
To the lonely sea and the sky,
And all I ask is a tall ship and a star to steer her by,
And the wheel's kick and the wind's song,
And the white sail's shaking,
And a grey mist on the sea's face and a grey dawn breaking.

John Masefield, *Sea Fever*

It was many and many a year ago,
In a kingdom by the sea,
That a maiden there lived whom you may know
By the name of Annabel Lee;
And this maiden she lived with no other thought
Than to love and be loved by me.

Edgar Allan Poe, *Annabel Lee*

When you stick your hand in a flowing stream, you touch the last that has gone before and the first of what is still to come.

Leonardo Da Vinci

Don't go chasing waterfalls

TLC

Yosemite National Park, CA

I am a sailor, you're my first mate
We signed on together, we coupled our fate
Hauled up our anchor determined not to fail
For the heart's treasure together we set sail
With no maps to guide us we steered our own course
We rode out the storms when the winds were gale force
Sat out the doldrums with patience and hope
Working together we learned how to cope
Life is an ocean and love is a boat
In troubled water it keeps us afloat
When we started the voyage
There was just me and you
Now gathered round us we have our own crew
Together we're in this relationship
We built it with care to last the whole trip
Our true destination's not marked on any chart
For we're navigating the shores of a heart
Life is an ocean and love is a boat
In troubled water it keeps us afloat
When we started the voyage
There was just me and you...
Now gathered round us we have our own crew

John McDermott

Jolly Rover, off Mallory Square
Key West, FL

Great Egret

Our Great Lakes, harbors, ports and rivers provide not only vital resources for us to live, but an entire maritime way of life for so many people. The least we can do is protect it, and the way of life it provides for so many.

Candice S. Miller, *U.S. Congress*

O Captain! My Captain!

Our fearful trip is done, the ship has weathered every rock,

the prize we sought is won, the port is near,

the bells I hear, the people all exulting.

Walt Whitman

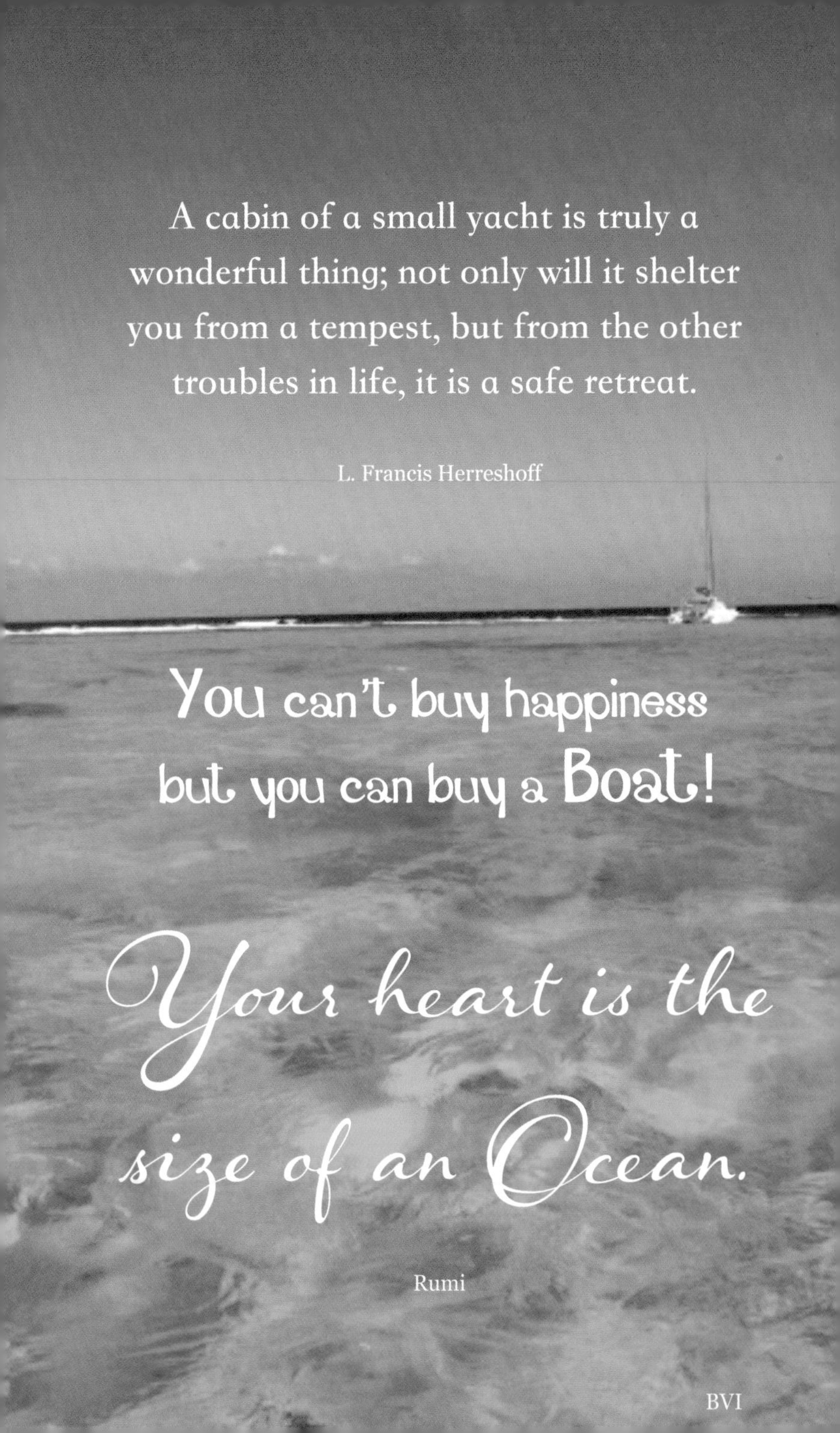

A cabin of a small yacht is truly a wonderful thing; not only will it shelter you from a tempest, but from the other troubles in life, it is a safe retreat.

L. Francis Herreshoff

You can't buy happiness but you can buy a Boat!

Your heart is the size of an Ocean.

Rumi

BVI

Many drops make a bucket, many buckets make a pond, many ponds make a lake, and many lakes make an ocean.

Percy Ross

Grandma's House

PERHAPS THE TRUTH DEPENDS ON A WALK AROUND THE LAKE.

Wallace Stevens

Hanalei Bay, HI

Puff, the Magic Dragon,

lived by the sea,

and frolicked in the autumn mist

in a land called Honalee.

Peter Yarrow & Lenny Lipton

When I sell liquor, it's called bootlegging; when my patrons serve it on Lake Shore Drive, it's called hospitality.

Al Capone

Honduras

TO THE QUESTION, "WHEN WERE YOUR SPIRITS AT THE LOWEST EBB?" THE OBVIOUS ANSWER SEEMED TO BE, "WHEN THE GIN GAVE OUT."

Sir Francis Chichester

The Wreck of the Edmund Fitzgerald

The legend lives on from the Chippewa on down
Of the big lake they call Gitche Gumee
The lake, it is said, never gives up her dead
When the skies of November turn gloomy.

With a load of iron ore... 26,000 tons more
Than the Edmund Fitzgerald weighed empty
That good ship and crew was a bone to be chewed
When the gales of November came early.

Gordon Lightfoot, 1976

LAND WAS CREATED TO PROVIDE A PLACE FOR BOATS TO VISIT

Brooks Atkinson

Somewhere beyond the sea
Somewhere waiting for me
My lover stands on golden sands
And watches the ships that go sailing

Somewhere beyond the sea
She's there watching for me
If I could fly like birds on high
Then straight to her arms
I'd go sailing

Bobby Darin

Sittin' in the mornin' sun
I'll be sittin' when the evenin' come
Watching the ships roll in
And then I watch 'em roll away again, yeah

I'm sittin' on the dock of the bay
Watching the tide roll away
I'm just sittin' on the dock of the bay
Wastin' time

Otis Redding

Thing about boats is, you can always sell them if you don't like them. Can't sell kids.

Lin Pardey

If once you have slept on an island,
You'll never be quite the same.

Rachel Field

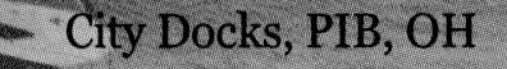

City Docks, PIB, OH

Sweet mother Michigan, father Superior
Coming down from Mackinac and Sault Ste. Marie
Blue water Huron, flow down to Lake Erie-O
Fall to Ontario and run on out to sea

Hearty are the seamen on the ships that load the iron ore
Sailing out of Thunder Bay and bound for Buffalo
Hearty are the fishermen just like their fathers were before
Say they'll bury me at sea come my time to go

Pat Dailey

Because there's nothing more beautiful than the way the ocean refuses to stop kissing the shoreline, no matter how many times it's sent away.

Sarah Kay

Jost Van Dyke, BVI

Bareboating, BVI

Oh the canvas can do miracles, just you wait and see...

Christopher Cross

Tall Ship Bowsprit

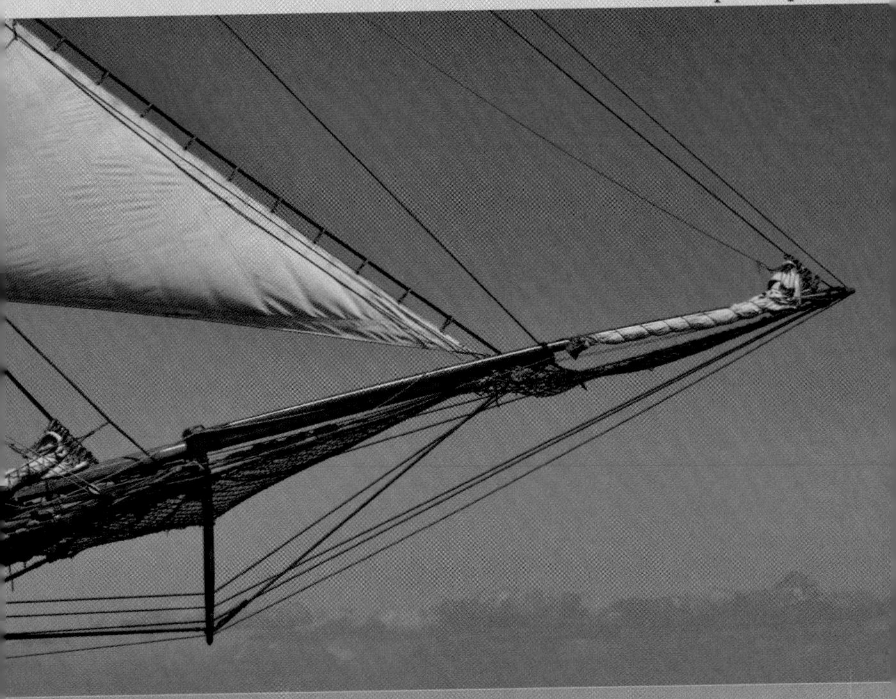

THAT'S WHAT A SHIP IS, YOU KNOW...
IT'S NOT JUST A KEEL AND A HULL
AND A DECK AND SAILS,
THAT'S WHAT A SHIP NEEDS.
BUT WHAT A SHIP IS,... REALLY IS, IS FREEDOM.

Captain Jack Sparrow, *Pirates of the Caribbean*

blessed are the curious
for they shall
have adventures

Loyelle Drachman

You can never cross the ocean
until you have the courage to
lose sight of the shore.

Christopher Columbus

A Sundog

Live in the sunshine,
Swim in the sea,
Drink the wild air.

Ralph Waldo Emerson

The sea is the same as it has been since before men ever went on it in boats.

Ernest Hemingway

Life is simple... just add water!

Kalalau Trail, Kauai, HI

Respect the Lake!

A smooth sea never made for a skilled sailor.

Off Rattlesnake Island, OH

I got my toes in the water, ass in the sand
Not a worry in the world, cold beer in my hand
Life is good today, life is good today

Zac Brown Band

Morada Bay, Islamorada, FL

Life is a beach, I'm just playin' in the sand.

Lil Wayne

Anini Beach, Kauai, HI

Taps

Day is done, gone the sun,
From the lakes, from the hills, from the skies.
All is well, safely rest,
God is nigh.

When the lights go down in the city
And the sun shines on the bay
Do I want to be there in my city

Journey

San Francisco Bay, CA

Mother,
Mother
Ocean...
I have heard
You call

Jimmy Buffett

Tow Line

Somewhere in Ireland

there are good ships, and
there are wood ships,
the ships that sail the sea.
but the best ships are
friendships,
and may they always be.

Irish Toast

Calypso

To sail on a dream on a crystal clear ocean
To ride on the crest of a wild raging storm
To work in the service of life and the living
In search of the answers to questions unknown
To be part of the movement and part of the growing
Part of beginning to understand

Aye, Calypso, the places you've been to
The things that you've shown us
The stories you tell
Aye, Calypso, I sing to your spirit
The men who have served you
So long and so well

Like the dolphin who guides you
You bring us beside you
To light up the darkness and show us the way
For though we are strangers in your silent world
To live on the land we must learn from the sea
To be true as the tide
And free as the wind swell
Joyful and loving in letting it be

John Denver, *Calypso*
In reference to Jacques Yves Cousteau's ship

Marathon, FL

Giverny, France

When was the last time you spent a quiet moment
just doing nothing. . . just sitting and looking
at the sea, or watching the wind blowing the tree limbs,
or watching the waves rippling on a pond,
a flickering candle or children playing in the park?

Ralph Marston

Got a whale of a tale to tell ya, lads
A whale of a tale or two
'Bout the flappin' fish and the girls I've loved
On nights like this with the moon above
A whale of a tale and it's all true
I swear by my tattoo

20,000 Leagues Under the Sea, Disney 1954

The world's finest wilderness lies beneath the waves...

Wyland

Joy to the fishes in the deep blue sea
Joy to you and me

Three Dog Night

Remember when you were my boat, and I was your sea, together we'd float so delicately.

You Me At Six

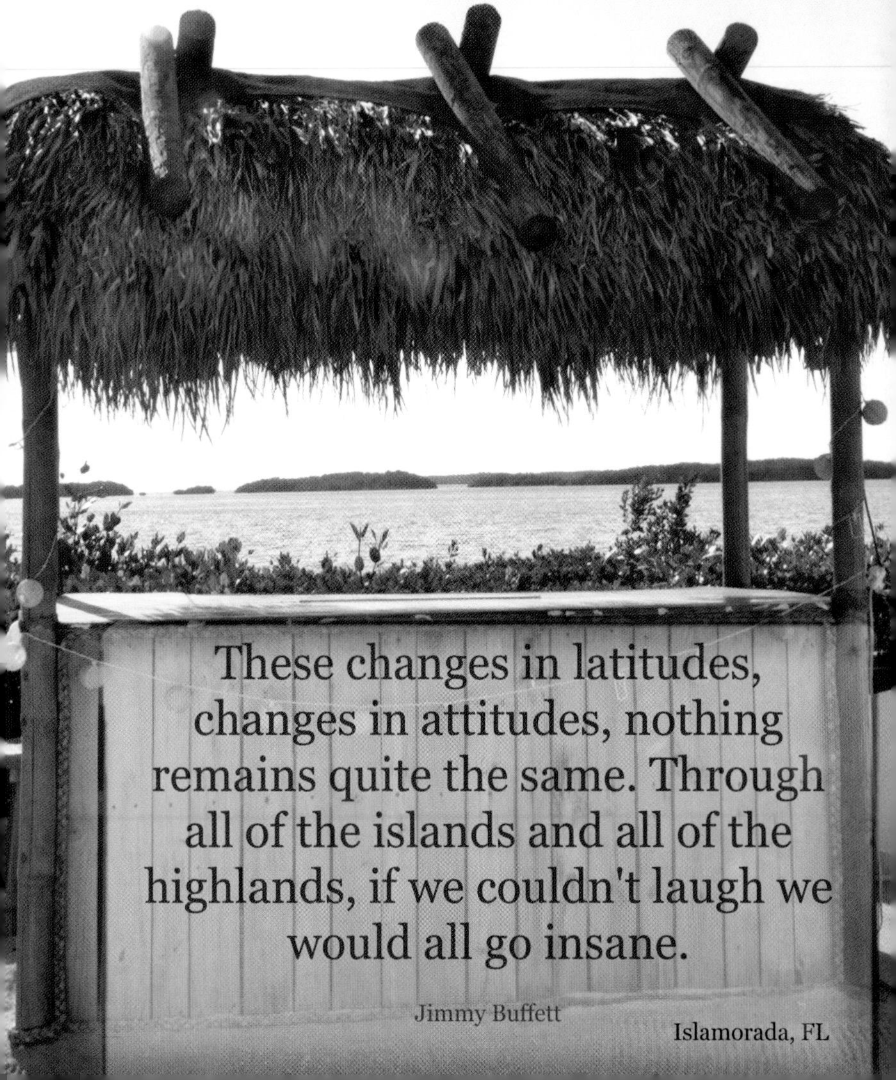

These changes in latitudes, changes in attitudes, nothing remains quite the same. Through all of the islands and all of the highlands, if we couldn't laugh we would all go insane.

Jimmy Buffett

Islamorada, FL

Locks of Love, over the Seine River, Paris, France

Life is like a river,

sometimes it sweeps you

gently along

and sometimes the rapids

come out of nowhere.

Emma Smith

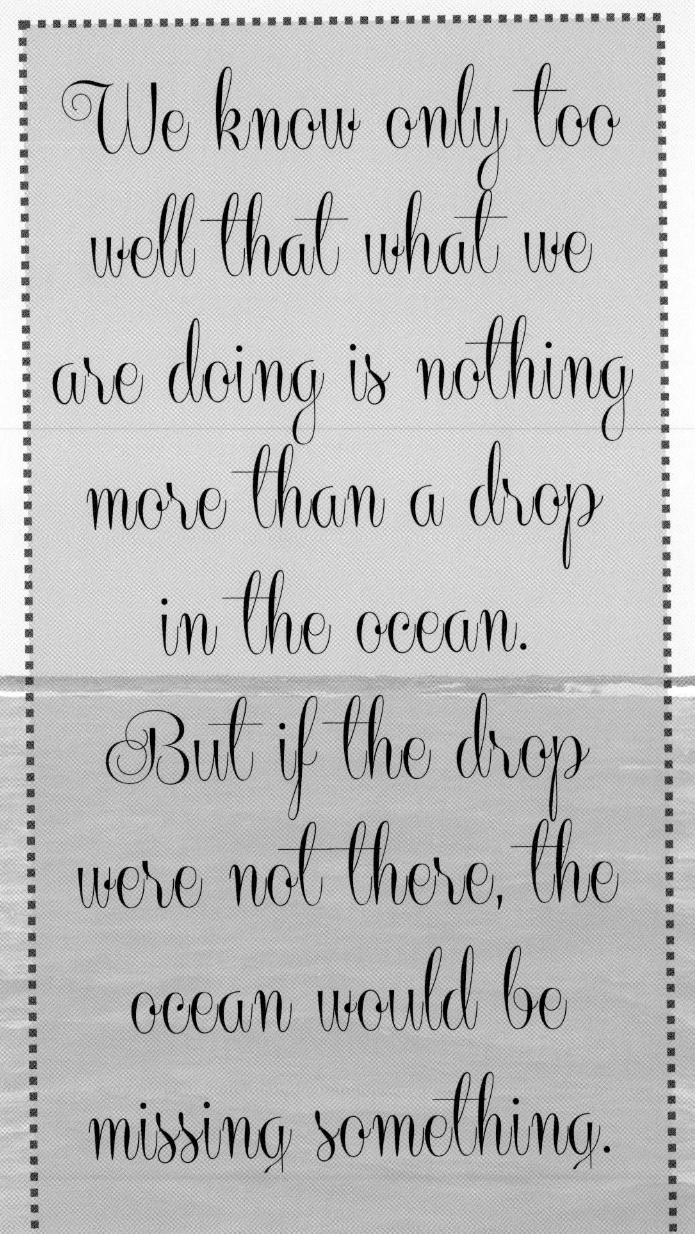

The Caribbean

God bless America, land that I love,
Stand beside her and guide her
Through the night with a light from above.
From the mountains, to the prairies,
To the oceans white with foam,
God bless America,
My home sweet home.

Irving Berlin

A ship is referred to as "she"
because it costs so much to keep
her in her paint and powder.

Admiral Chester W. Nimitz

Charleston, SC

Dominica,
Lesser Antilles

She sells seashells by the seashore.

To find a seashell is to discover a world of imagination.

Michelle Held

Bantry Bay, Ireland

Genesis 6:19-20 - And of every living thing of all flesh, two of every [sort] shalt thou bring into the ark, to keep [them] alive with thee; they shall be male and female.

Moses?

Happiness is a summer breeze,
Sand between your toes,
And your best friend by your side

Anonymous

Arch Rock, Mackinac Island, MI

BIG LAKE SMALL ISLAND

On an island in the sun
We'll be playin' an' havin' fun
And it makes me feel so fine
I can't control my brain

Weezer

If your ship doesn't come in, swim out to meet it.

Jonathan Winters

Life's a reach… then you jibe.

Annapolis, MD

I am not afraid of storms for I am learning how to sail my ship.

Louisa May Alcott

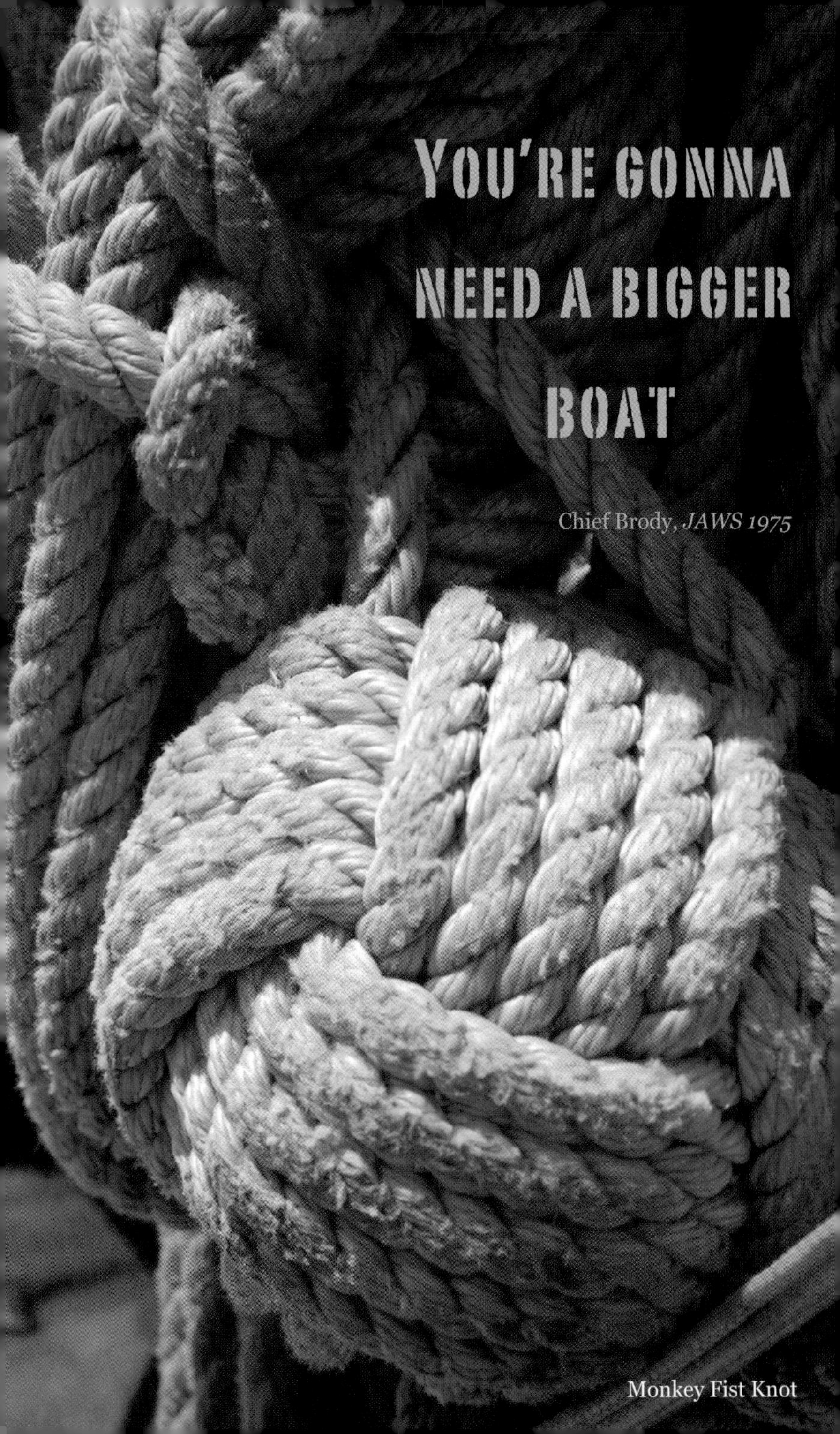

YOU'RE GONNA NEED A BIGGER BOAT

Chief Brody, *JAWS 1975*

Monkey Fist Knot

Carriacou Boat Yard, Grenada

TAKE ME TO THE RIVER
DROP ME IN THE WATER

Talking Heads

When I forget how talented God is, I look to the sea.

Whoopi Goldberg

The cure for anything is salt water~ sweat, tears, or the sea.

Isak Dinesen

Mona Island,
Puerto Rico

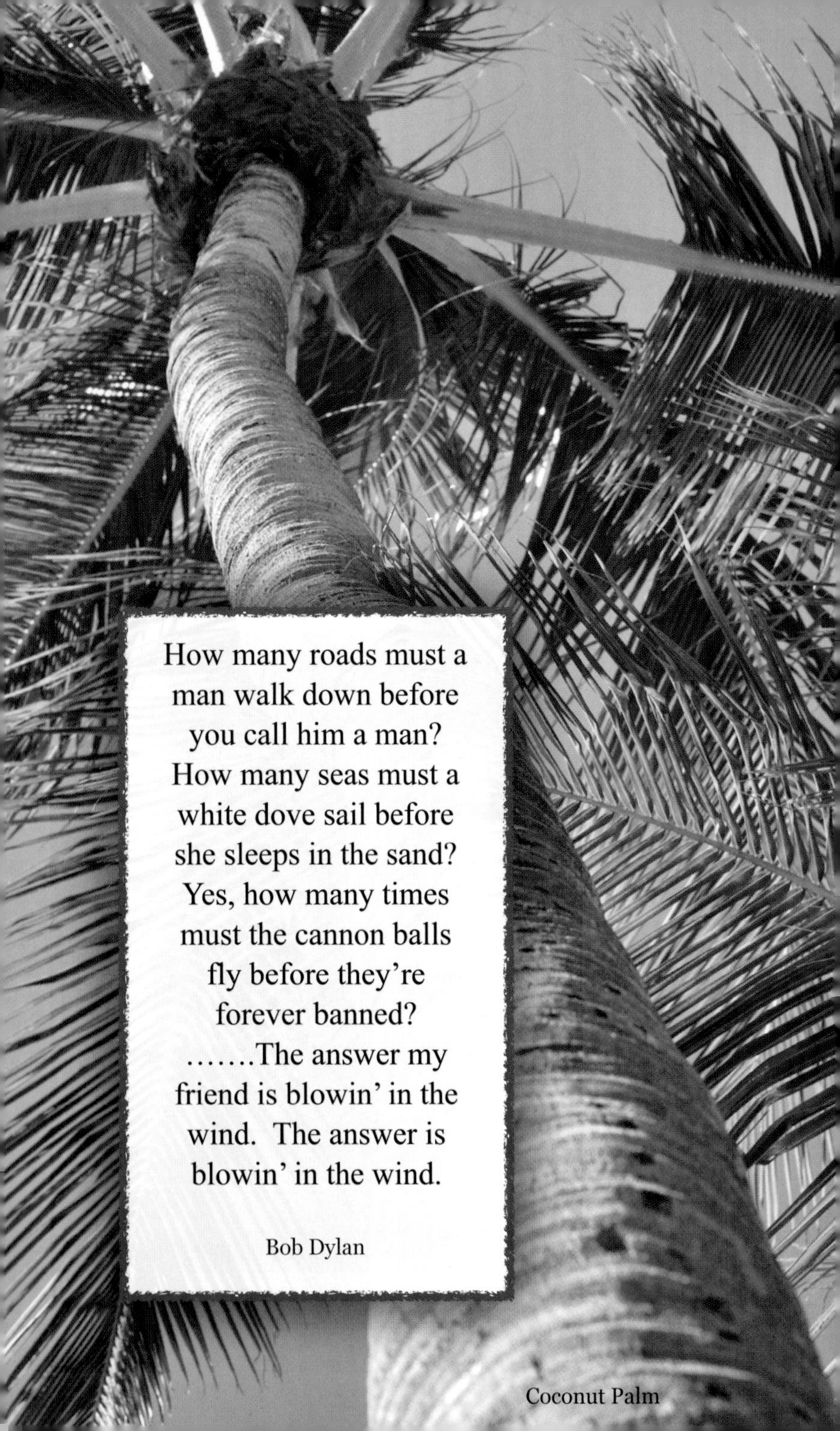

How many roads must a
man walk down before
you call him a man?
How many seas must a
white dove sail before
she sleeps in the sand?
Yes, how many times
must the cannon balls
fly before they're
forever banned?
.......The answer my
friend is blowin' in the
wind. The answer is
blowin' in the wind.

Bob Dylan

Coconut Palm

You are the only fish in the sea for me!

Georgia Aquarium, Atlanta, GA

One Fish
Two Fish
Red Fish
Blue Fish

Dr. Seuss

Duck Key, FL

A LOT OF PEOPLE ATTACK THE SEA, I MAKE LOVE TO IT.

Jacques Yves Cousteau

Earth and sky,
woods and fields,
lakes and rivers,
the mountain
and the sea,
are excellent
schoolmasters, and
teach some of us
more than we can
ever learn from
books.

John Lubbock

East Point, PIB, OH

Human nature is like water. It takes the shape of its container.

Wallace Stevens

the more clearly we can focus our attention on the wonders and realities of the universe about us, the less taste we shall have for destruction.

Rachel Carson

One doesn't discover new lands without consenting to lose sight of the shore...

André Gide

Carriacou Island, Grenada

Underway for St. Eustatius

The sea, once it casts its spell, holds one in its net of wonder forever.

Jacque Yves Cousteau

Though pleas'd to see dolphins at play, I mind my compass and my way.

Matthew Green

THE STARFISH

One day a man was walking along the shore and saw a young child picking up something and gently throwing it into the ocean.

As he got closer he called out, “Good morning, what are you doing?

The young child paused, looked up and replied, “Throwing starfish into the ocean.”

The man asked, “Why are you throwing starfish into the ocean?”

“The sun is up and the tide is going out. If I don’t throw them back, they’ll die.”

“But, young child, don’t you realize that there are miles and miles of beach and starfish all along it. You can’t possibly make a difference.”

The young child listened politely, then bent down, picked up another starfish and threw it back into the sea and said, “I made a difference to that one.”

Unknown

Half Moon Bay, CA

Our memories of the ocean will linger on... long after our footprints in the sand are gone.

Unknown

At the beach, life is different. Time doesn't move hour to hour but mood to moment. We live by the currents, plan by the tides, and follow the sun.

Sandy Gingras

IT'S
ONLY
IN
THE
WIDE
OPEN
SPACES
THAT
WE
FIND
OURSELVES
Honduras

St. Lucia

Do I love you? My God, if your love were a grain of sand, mine would be a universe of beaches.

Wesley to Buttercup, *The Princess Pride, 1987*

A real friend is someone who takes a winter vacation on a sun~drenched beach and does not send a card.

Farmer's Almanac

I started early, took my dog,
And visited the sea~
The Mermaids in the basement
Came out to look at me. . .

Emily Dickinson

~ Near Alligator Reef, PIB, OH

Beauty in the water
Angel on the beach
Ocean's daughter. . .

Train

Florida Keys

Song of a Shell

I held a sea shell to my ear,
And listened to its tale
Of vessels bounding o'er the main
And all the ships that sail.
It sang of brilliant water flowers—
The bright anemones
That bloom beneath the ocean waves—
Tossed in from seven seas.
Each time I harken to this song,
I hear the breakers moan,
And fancy that a warning bell
Rings from a lighthouse lone.
No longer need I wish to go
Where foam-capped billows swell,
For I've an ocean of my own
Within this pearly shell.

Violet L. Cuslidge

I could never stay long enough on the shore; the tang of the untainted, fresh, and free sea air was like a cool, quieting thought...

Helen Keller

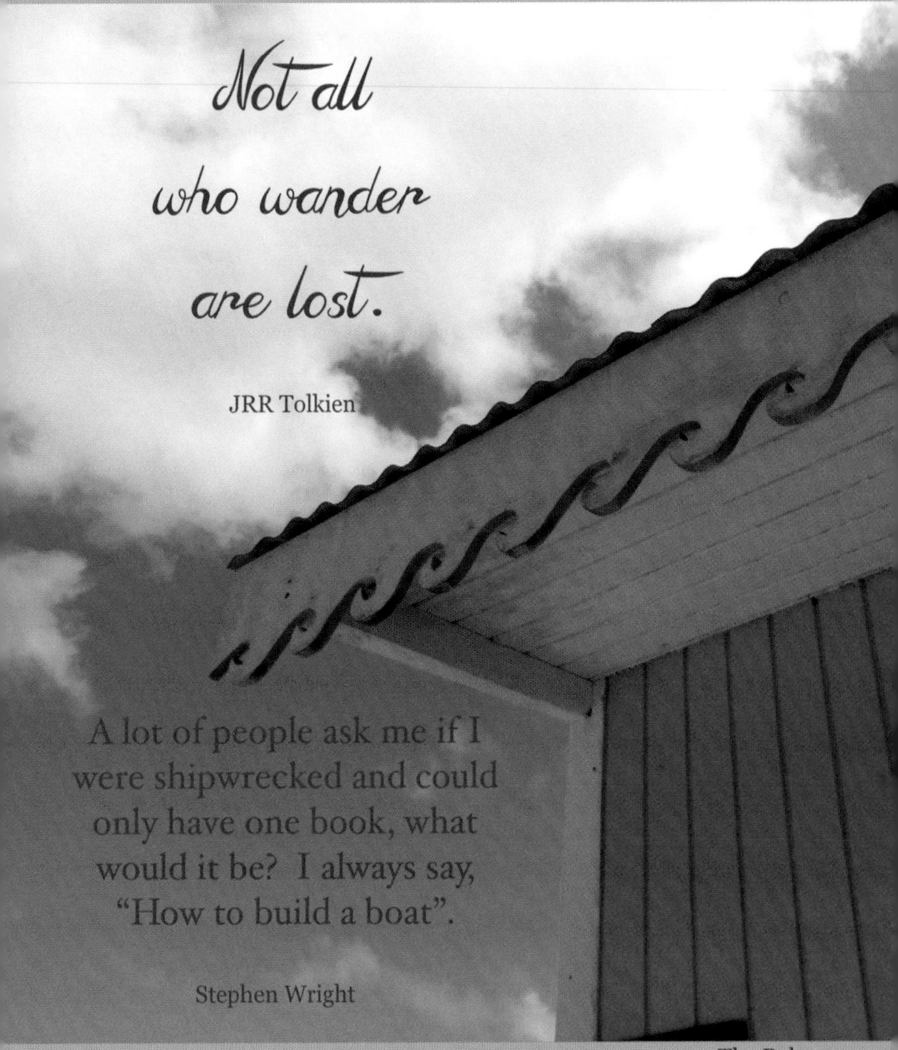

Not all who wander are lost.

JRR Tolkien

A lot of people ask me if I were shipwrecked and could only have one book, what would it be? I always say, "How to build a boat".

Stephen Wright

The Bahamas

The fishermen know that the sea is dangerous and the storm is terrible, but they have never found these dangers sufficient reason for remaining ashore.

Vincent Van Gogh

Creativity is the Blue Heron within us waiting to fly; through her imagination, all things become possible.

Nadia Janice Brown

Squaw Harbor, PIB, OH

Home is where the
waves are

You must not lose faith in humanity. Humanity is an ocean; if a few drops of the ocean are dirty, the ocean does not become dirty.

Mahatma Gandhi

Grand Cayman

My job, my mission, the reason
I have been put on this planet,
is to save wildlife.

Steve Irwin

Listen, Miss, boats are supposed to float. Even if they break up, they usually still float and show up on a shore somewhere.

Cathy Ostlere

Vessels large may venture more, but little boats should keep near shore.

Benjamin Franklin

AMERICA! AMERICA!
GOD SHED HIS GRACE ON THEE,
AND CROWN THY GOOD WITH
BROTHERHOOD,
FROM SEA TO SHINING SEA.

Katherine Lee Bates

Tall Ship & Old Glory

There's nothing... absolutely nothing... half so much worth doing as messing about in boats.

Kenneth Grahame, *The Wind in the Willows*

ILYA Jr. Regatta, Great Lakes

WE MAY ALL HAVE COME ON DIFFERENT SHIPS, BUT WE'RE IN THE SAME BOAT NOW.

Martin Luther King, Jr.

The days pass happily with me whenever my ship sails.

Captain Joshua Slocum

A reel fisherman can tackle anything!

EARLY TO BED
EARLY TO RISE
FISH ALL DAY
MAKE UP LIES

Newport, RI

Cocoa Beach, FL

If Love was
Water,
I'd give you the

Unknown

PIBCSS Sailing Class, off Gibraltar Island, OH

“Now then, Pooh," said Christopher Robin, "where's your boat?"
"I ought to say," explained Pooh as they walked down to the shore of the island, "that it isn't just an ordinary sort of boat. Sometimes it's a Boat, and sometimes it's more of an Accident. It all depends."
"Depends on what?"
"On whether I'm on the top of it or underneath it.”

A.A. Milne, *Winnie the Pooh*

Chesapeake Bay

TO FISH OR NOT TO FISH ??
WHAT A STUPID QUESTION !

Rock the Boat

Ever since our voyage of love began...Your touch has thrilled me like the rush of the wind... And your arms have held me safe from a rolling sea...There's always been a quiet place to harbor you and me.

Our love is like a ship on the ocean... We've been sailing with a cargo full of, love and devotion.

So I'd like to know where, you got the notion... Said I'd like to know where, you got the notion.

To rock the boat, don't rock the boat, baby
rock the boat, don't tip the boat over.

Hues Corporation

Rock Stacking & Balancing
Lake Huron Shore, MI

The seaweed is always greener in somebody else's lake.

The Little Mermaid, *Disney 1989*

She's Elusive, Rides the Waves of Life
Kisses by the Light of the Moon
& Respects the Lake

Sara Booker

Freshwater Mermaid
Great Lakes

HARK, NOW HEAR
THE SAILORS CRY,
SMELL THE SEA,
AND FEEL THE SKY
LET YOUR SOUL &
SPIRIT FLY, INTO
THE MYSTIC...

Van Morrison

Old Fish Floats

Wyland

Loggerhead sea turtle release, M.M. 88 Restaurant 2.14.14
Turtle Rehabilitation at The Turtle Hospital, Marathon, FL

If others want to define you, don't linger in their pond. Swim away from their ignorance and find your ocean.

Dodinsky

Kauai, HI, Pacific Ocean

Water, water, everywhere,
Nor any drop to drink.

Samuel Taylor Coleridge, *The Rime of the Ancient Mariner*

U.S. Brig Niagara, Schoolhouse Bay,
Middle Bass Island, OH

Wisdom Sails with Wind and Time

John Florio

LINNE: A Gaelic term used for pool, pond, lake, or sea.

Bantry Bay, Ireland

First You Have to Row a Little Boat

Richard Bode

Bad cooking is responsible for more trouble at sea than all other things put together.

Thomas Fleming Day

Should you find yourself in a chronically leaking boat, energy devoted to changing vessels is likely to be more productive than energy devoted to patching leaks.

Warren Buffett

Georgia Aquarium, Atlanta, GA

WHAT WOULD AN OCEAN
BE WITHOUT A MONSTER
LURKING IN THE DARK?
IT WOULD BE LIKE SLEEP
WITHOUT DREAMS.

Werner Herzog

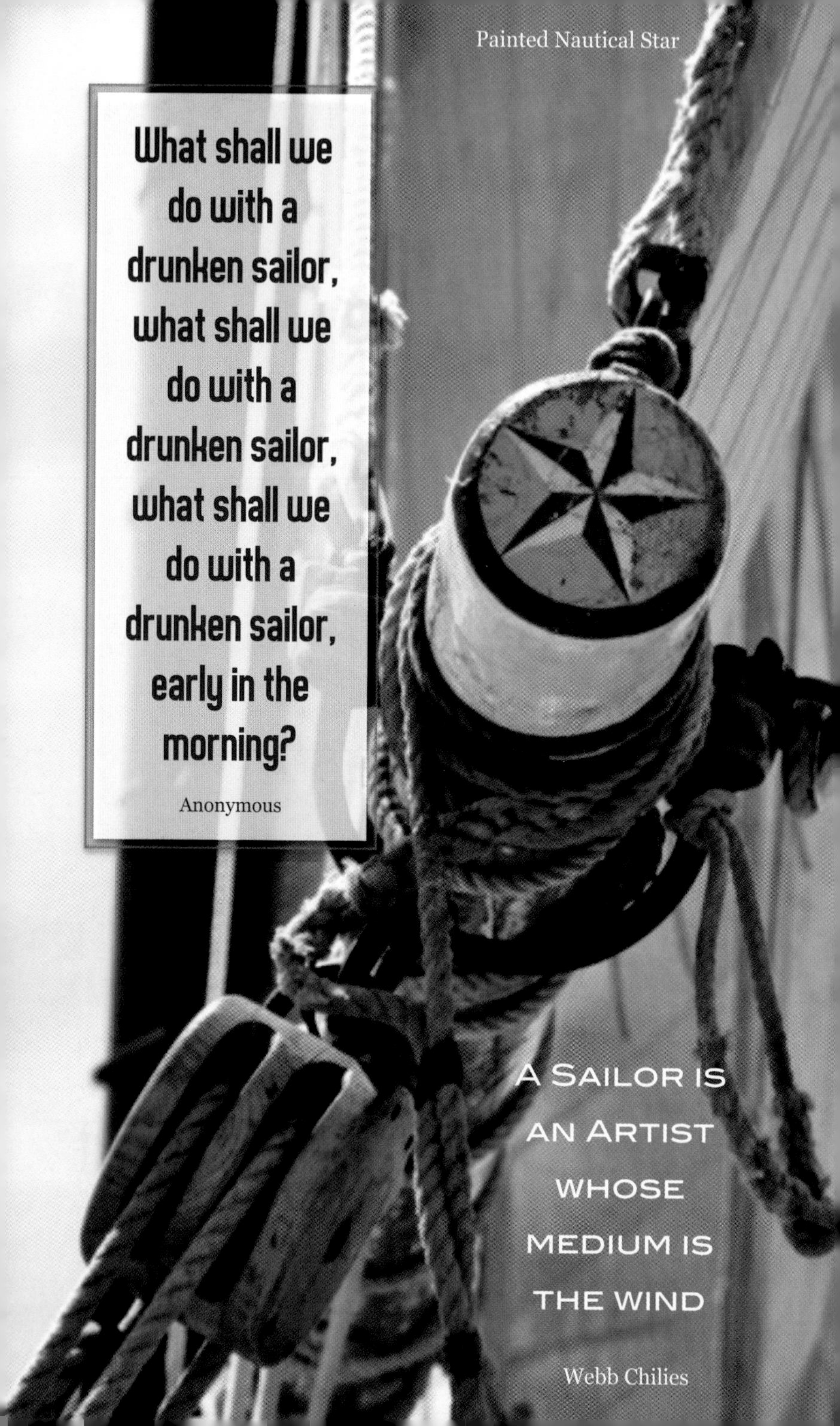

Painted Nautical Star

What shall we do with a drunken sailor, what shall we do with a drunken sailor, what shall we do with a drunken sailor, early in the morning?

Anonymous

A SAILOR IS AN ARTIST WHOSE MEDIUM IS THE WIND

Webb Chilies

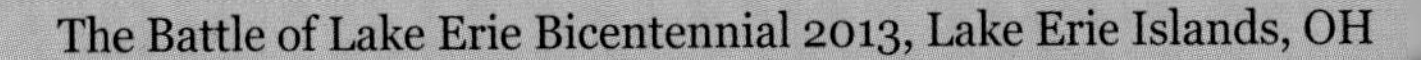
The Battle of Lake Erie Bicentennial 2013, Lake Erie Islands, OH

We have met the enemy and they are ours:
Two Ships, two Brigs, one Schooner and one Sloop.

Oliver Hazard Perry

When I look into your eyes
It's like watching the night sky
Or a beautiful sunrise
There's so much they hold
And just like them old stars
I see that you've come so far
To be right where you are
How old is your soul?

I won't give up on us
Even if the skies get rough
I'm giving you all my love
I'm still looking up

And when you're needing your space
To do some navigating
I'll be here patiently waiting
To see what you find

Jason Mraz

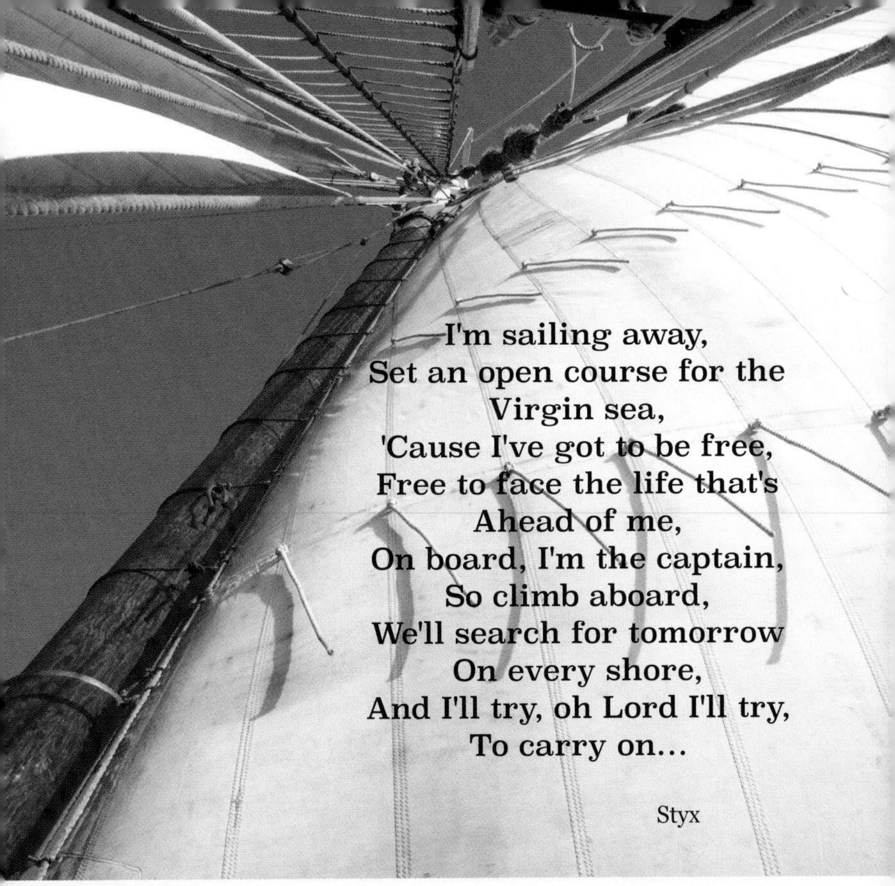

I'm sailing away,
Set an open course for the
Virgin sea,
'Cause I've got to be free,
Free to face the life that's
Ahead of me,
On board, I'm the captain,
So climb aboard,
We'll search for tomorrow
On every shore,
And I'll try, oh Lord I'll try,
To carry on...

Styx

Wooden Mast & Mainsail

Sail away with me honey
I put my heart in your hands
Sail away with me honey now, now, now
Sail away with me
What will be will be
I want to hold you now

David Gray

boat |bōt| noun

1 a small vessel propelled on water by oars, sails, or an engine: *a fishing boat* | [as modifier] *: a boat trip*.

• (in general use) a ship of any size.

Winch & Lines

That's what sailing is, a dance, and your partner is the sea. And with the sea you never take liberties. You ask her, you don't tell her. You have to remember always that she's the leader, not you. You and your boat are dancing to her tune.

Michael Morpurgo,

Whatever Floats Your Boat

Roatán, Honduras

Life is a shipwreck, but we must not forget to sing in the lifeboats.

Voltaire

Wine Hath Drowned More Men Than the Sea

Thomas Fuller

Contributors & Credits

~~~~~~

1. Our Anchors are the people in our lives that we will be forever attached... and you know who you are! .....and thank you "m"!
2. Information. * If there is no known contributor than the quote may remain un~credited. Then 2 blank pages.
3. Unknown & for bigger boats it's "Ten Thousand". From K.W.
4. Robert N. Rose, *My Ship O'Dreams.* Woody Guthrie, 1912~1967, American singer/songwriter and folk musician.
5. Kate Chopin, 1851~1904, *The Awakening,* 1899.
6. Edward Gibbon, 1737~1794, English historian and writer.
7. Unknown. Sir Knox Johnston, b. 1939, English sailor. In 1968 he became the first man to perform a single~handed non~stop circumnavigation of the globe. Unknown.
8. Sara Booker, artist. James S. Tippett, 1885~1958, American educator and children's writer.
9. James Lawrence, American Navel Officer quote: 1813. Francis Scott Key, 1779~1843, American lawyer, author, and poet.
10. Just Great Memories! Bareboating is one of the best experiences a family can have...
11. Written by Zach Berkman, songwriter & author, along with Ron Pope, American singer~songwriter. Hammond Innes,1913~1998, British novelist.
12. Buzzy Trent, 1929~2006, American pioneer of big wave surfing. Anne Morrow~Lindbergh, 1906~2001, *A Gift from the Sea,* pioneering American aviator, author, and wife of Charles Lindbergh.
13. Gilligan's Island, Sherwood Schwartz, writer & George Wyle, composer.
14. Anais Nin, 1903~1977, French~born author. Jack Booker, nephew & godson. JFK, *Newport dinner speech before America's Cup Races,* 1962.
15. Chinese Proverb, thanks China! Just combined a few statements.~~I try.
16. R.D. Culler, 1909~1978, American navel architect. Roselle Mercier Montgomery, 1874~1933, American poetress. E.B. White, 1899~1985, American writer.
17. *Titanic,* 1997, written, directed, co~produced, co~edited, and co~financed by James Cameron. Gilda Radner, 1946~1989, American comedian and actress. Erma Bombeck, 1927~1996, American humorist and author.
18. Performed by: The Drifters, 1964. Songwriters: Arthur Resnick, Kenny Young.
19. Old English Proverb, thank you Europe! *Pirates of the Caribbean, 2003, Disney*
20. William Johnson Corey, 1823~1892, British poet. Ella Wheeler Wilcox, American author and poet. Wow...she was amazing!
21. Unknown. Francis Stokes, 1926~2008, American sailor and author, *The Moonshine Logs.*
22. Sara Booker, artist. Barry Cornwall, 1787~1874, English poet.
23. Steve Jobs, 1955~2011, American businessman, innovator, and entrepreneur. Unknown.
24. *Peter Pan in Kensington Gardens* by J.M. Barrie.
25. Tamora Pierce, 1953, American writer, *Sandry's Book.*
26. William Shakespeare, 1564~1616, British playwright and poet. Doug Larson, b. 1926, American writer. Mark Twain, 1835~1910, American novelist and humorist.
27. Heinrich Zimmer, 1890~1943, Indologist and historian of South Asian art. Native American wisdom is always captivating!
28. Jack Johnson, b. 1975, American folk rock singer/songwriter, professional surfer, and filmmaker. Unknown.
29. Bertha W. Calloway, b. 1925. African~American writer, historian, and community activist. ~ several variations. Mark Twain, 1835~1910, American novelist and humorist.
30. Jimmy Buffett, b. 1946, American singer/songwriter, author and businessman.
31. Henry J. Tillman, 1847~1918, American politician. Jokes are unknown.
32. Loren Eiseley, 1907~1977, American anthropologist, educator, philosopher, and natural science writer.
33. Bob Bitchin, Facebook/Bob~Bitchin, *Cruising Outpost,* American publisher, writer, and sailor. Chris McCandless, 1968~1992, American hiker who ventured out into the Alaskan wilderness. His story inspired the book, *Into the Wild,* written by Jon Krakauer and adapted the movie, *Into the Wild* by Sean Penn.
34. William Atkin, 1882~1962, sailboat designer . *SpongeBob SquarePants,* composed by Hank Smith Music, voice of Patrick Pinney, creator, Stephen Hillinburg.
Kid Rock, b. 1971, American multi~instrumentalist, music producer, and actor.
35. Thomas Hardy, 1840~1928, English novelist and poet. Play on words quote.
36. Anonymous? Hint: b. 1967 and still acts like a teenager, to many tools to count. Old Sailors Proverb flows so nicely. Lin and Larry Pardey, a married couple in their 70's that have sailed over 200,000 miles together and have circumnavigated the world both east~about and west~about. A fascinating couple worth reading about. *If you need glasses to read this~ we're getting old.
~~~~~~

37. Charles Wysocki, 1928~2002, Americana folk painter. *The Lighthouse's Tale,* performed by Nickel Creek, written by Adam McKenzie and Chris Thile.
38. St. Patrick, enough said! Be green!
39. Ahhh ... a good laugh had by all. I did ride those waves and said that.
Henry Wadsworth Longfellow, 1807~1882, American poet.
40. Sally B.S., an alter~ego. Unknown.
41. Finnish Proverb, hope to make it there someday.
Henry David Thoreau, 1817~1862, American author, poet and philosopher.
42. Willa Cather, 1873~1947, among the most eminent American authors.
43. George S. Patton, 1885~1945, United States Army general. Robert Frost, 1874~1963, American poet. Preben Sejer Kristensen, Owner and CEO of The Dragon Project Ltd. and Green Explorers Society Ltd.
44. Billy Joel, b. 1949, American pianist, singer/songwriter, and composer. Touching lyrics.
45. Performed by The Beach Boys, written by Chuck Berry.
46. Both quotes are unknown.
47. Guys in college used to say "fish on". Anacharsis, 6th~ century BC. Henry Wheeler Shaw, 1818~1885, American humorist.
48. Just a great black & white photo.
49. Herman Melville, 1819~1891, American novelist and poet, *Moby Dick,* 1851.
Brandy, performed by Looking Glass, written by Elliot Lurie.
50. Zenna Schaffer, planner at *Joyfulnoise*, writer and humorist.
Ernest Hemingway, 1899~1961, American author and journalist.
Herbert Hoover, 1874~1964, 31st President of the United States.
51. John Masefield, 1878~1967, English poet and writer. Edgar Allan Poe, 1809~1849, American author, poet, editor and literary critic.
52. Leonardo Da Vinci, 1452~1519, Italian Renaissance genius.
Don't Go Chasing Waterfalls, performed by TLC, written by Lisa Lopes, Marqueze Ethridge, Rico Wade, Ray Murray, and Patrick Brown.
53. John McDermott, b. 1955, Scottish~Canadian tenor, *Love is a Voyage*. You Tube this song!
54. Candice S. Miller, b. 1954, U.S. Representative for Michigan's 10th congressional district.
Walt Whitman, 1819~1892, American poet, essayist, and journalist.
55. L. Francis Herreshoff, 1890~1972, Navel architect, boat designer, and author. Unknown. ~ so true. Rumi, 1207~1273, 13th~century Persian poet, jurist, theologian, and Sufi mystic.
56. Percy Ross, 1916~2001, American self~made multi~millionaire, philanthropist, and columnist. Cool story. Wallace Stevens, 1879~1955, American Modernist poet.
57. Peter Yarrow and Lenny Lipton wrote: *Puff the Magic Dragon,* performed by Peter, Paul and Mary, 1963.
58. Al Capone, 1899~1947, American gangster who led a Prohibition~era crime syndicate.
Sir Francis Chichester, 1901~1972, English aviator and sailor.
59. Gordon Lightfoot, b. 1938, Canadian singer/songwriter. Brooks Atkinson, 1894~1984, American theatre critic. What a life this man lived.
60. *Beyond the Sea*, written by Jack Lawrence, composed by Charles Trent, 1946, performed by Bobby Darin, 1959. *Sitting on the Dock of the Bay,* 1968, performed by Otis Redding and written by Steve Cropper and Otis Redding.
61. Lin Pardey, b. 1944, Sailor, author, and amazing woman. Worth reading about.
62. Rachel Field, 1894~1942, American novelist, poet and children's writer.
Pat Dailey, American folksinger/songwriter. Great guy!
63. Sarah Kay, American poet. *"B"*and *No Matter the Wreckage,* are her published books.
Very inspirational and talented.
64. *Sailing,* written by Brunwell Carter and performed by Christopher Cross, b. 1951.
65. *Disney, Pirates of the Caribbean*, Captain Jack Sparrow. Lovelle Drachman, Inspirational writer.
66. Christopher Columbus, 1450~1506, Italian explorer, navigator, and colonizer.
Ralph Waldo Emerson, 1803~1882, American essayist, lecturer, and poet.
67. Ernest Hemingway, 1899~1961, American author and journalist. Unknown.
68. All three expressions are unknown.
69. Zac Brown Band, *Toes,* 2008, co~written by Zac Brown, John Driskell Hopkins, Shawn Mullins, and Wyatt Durette.
70. Lil Wayne, b. 1982, American rapper. Middle daughter is a huge fan and tries to rap like him.
71. *Taps,* several versions~ this one, unknown. *Lights*, 1978, performed by Journey, written by Neal Schon and Steve Perry.
72. Jimmy Buffett, 1946, American singer/songwriter, author, & businessman.
73. Irish Toast, this is my favorite version and all children should learn this!
74. John Denver, 1943~1997, Singer/songwriter and so much more. The *Calypso* lyrics bring tears to my eyes. Had the pleasure to see him in concert.

75. Ralph Marston, b. 1955, American writer.
76. Kirk Douglas performs dance & song in film. Wyland, American multi~faceted artist, educator, scuba diver, conservationist and explorer. *Joy to the World*, performed by Three Dog Night and written by Hoyt Axton.
77. You Me At Six, British rock band. Jimmy Buffett, his lyrics define summer.
78. Emma Smith, 1804~1879, first President of the Relief Society.
79. Mother Teresa, 1910~1997, Roman Catholic Religious Sister and missionary.
80. Irving Berlin, 1888~1989, American composer and lyricist. Admiral Chester W. Nimitz, 1885~ 1966, Fleet Admiral of the U.S. Navy.
81. Unknown tongue~twister. Michelle Held, writer, inspirationalist.
82. Genesis, this is no musical band. Moses? Unknown.
83. Just made it up. *Island in the Sun*, performed by Weezer, written by Rivers Cuomo.
84. Jonathan Winters, 1925~2013, American actor, comedian, and artist. Unknown. Louisa May Alcott, 1832~1888, American novelist.
85. *JAWS,* 1975 , written by Peter Benchley, directed by Steven Spielberg. Favorite movie ever.
86. Talking Heads , *Take me to the River*, written by Al Green and Mabon Hodges, 1974. Whoopi Goldberg, b. 1955, American comedian, actor & author. Rent *Sister Act,* if you haven't seen it.
87. Isak Dinesen, 1885~1962, Danish writer.
88. Bob Dylan, 1941, American musician, singer/songwriter, artist and writer.
89. Unknown. Dr. Seus, 1904~1991, American writer, poet, and cartoonist.
90. Jacque Yves Cousteau, 1910~1997, French naval officer, explorer, conservationist, filmmaker, innovator, scientist, photographer, and author.
91. John Lubbock, English author, *The Pleasures of Life.*
92. Wallace Stevens, 1879~1955, American poet. Rachel Carson, 1907~1964, American marine biologist, conservationist and author, *Silent Spring.*
93. Andre Gide, 1869~1951, French author.
94. Jacque Yves Cousteau, pg. 90. Matthew Green, 1696~1737, British poet.
95. Unknown. Half Moon Bay is spectacular and worth a trip, if going to the west coast.
96. Unknown. Sandy Gingras, author and illustrator. Amazing woman in history.
97. Unknown. 98. *The Princess Bride*, 1987, written by William Goldman, directed by Rob Reiner. Farmers Almanac 21;45. Nearly impossible with social media.
99. Emily Dickinson, 1830~1886, American poet. Photo: Ellen Snyder, Josie Sheehan, Roxy, Audrey Sheehan, & Scotch. Train, *Mermaid,* 2012, written by Monahan, lind, Bjorklund, Hermansen, and Eriksen.
100. Violet L Cuslidge, poet. 101. Helen Keller, 1880~1968, American author. JRR Tolkien. Stephen Wright, b. 1955, American comedian, actor and author. Funnnnnny!
102. Vinvent Van Gogh, 1853~1890, Dutch painter. Nadia Janice Brown, writer and poet, *Unscrambled Eggs* and *The Life & Musings of a Girl Poet.*
103. Unknown. 104. Mahatma Gandhi, 1869~1948, Indian leader. Steve Irwin, 1962~2006, *The Crocodile Hunter,* Australian wildlife expert. A family favorite.
105. Cathy Ostlere, Canadian author, *Lost.* Benjamin Franklin, you can see him on the one~hundred dollar bill. 106. Katherine Lee Bates, 1859~1929, American songwriter. 107. Kenneth Grahame, 1859~1932, Scottish writer. Martin Luther King, Jr., 1929~1968, leader in the African~American Civil Rights Movement. Thank God for Martin!
108. Captain Joshua Slocum, 1844~1909, first man to sail single~handedly around the world. Later he was lost at sea. Unknown.
109. Unknown. 110. A.A. Miline, 1882~1956, English author. Andera Stevens. 111. Unknown.
112. *Rock the Boat,* 1973, written by Rapture D. Stewart, Eric L Seats, and Stephen Garrett.
113. *The Little Mermaid, Disney*, 1989. Sara Booker, in reference to a Freshwater Mermaid. Unknown. 114. Van Morrison, Northern Irish singer/songwriter, *Into the Mystic,* 1970.
115. Wyland, pg. 76. Dodinsky, *In The Garden of Thoughts*. Buy this book ...so cute.
116. Samuel Taylor Coleridge, 1772~1834, English poet.
117. Lister Sinclair, 1921~2006, Canadian broadcaster and playwright. John Florio, 1553~1625, royal language tutor at the Court of James 1.
118. Richard Bode, American author. Thomas Fleming Day,1 861~1927, founding editor of the *Rudder*. Warren Buffett, b. 1930, American business magnate.
119. Werner Herzog, German film director. 120. Anonymous. Webb Chillies, great sailor.
121. Oliver Hazard Perry, 1785~1819, American navel commander. Unknown.
122. Jason Mraz, b. 1977, American singer/songwriter. One of my favorite lyrics ever.
123. Styx, *Come Sail Away*, 1977. David Gray, b. 1968, British singer.
124. Michael Morpurgo,b. 1943, English author and poet, *Alone On A Wide Wide Sea.*
125. Unknown. Voltaire, 1694~1778, French writer, historian, and philosopher.

~If there is a comment following a credit, it's simply my opinion. A Sea of Thanks for reading and looking forward to the second edition. If you have a favorite quote for #2, I'd love for you to share. ~ Sara.